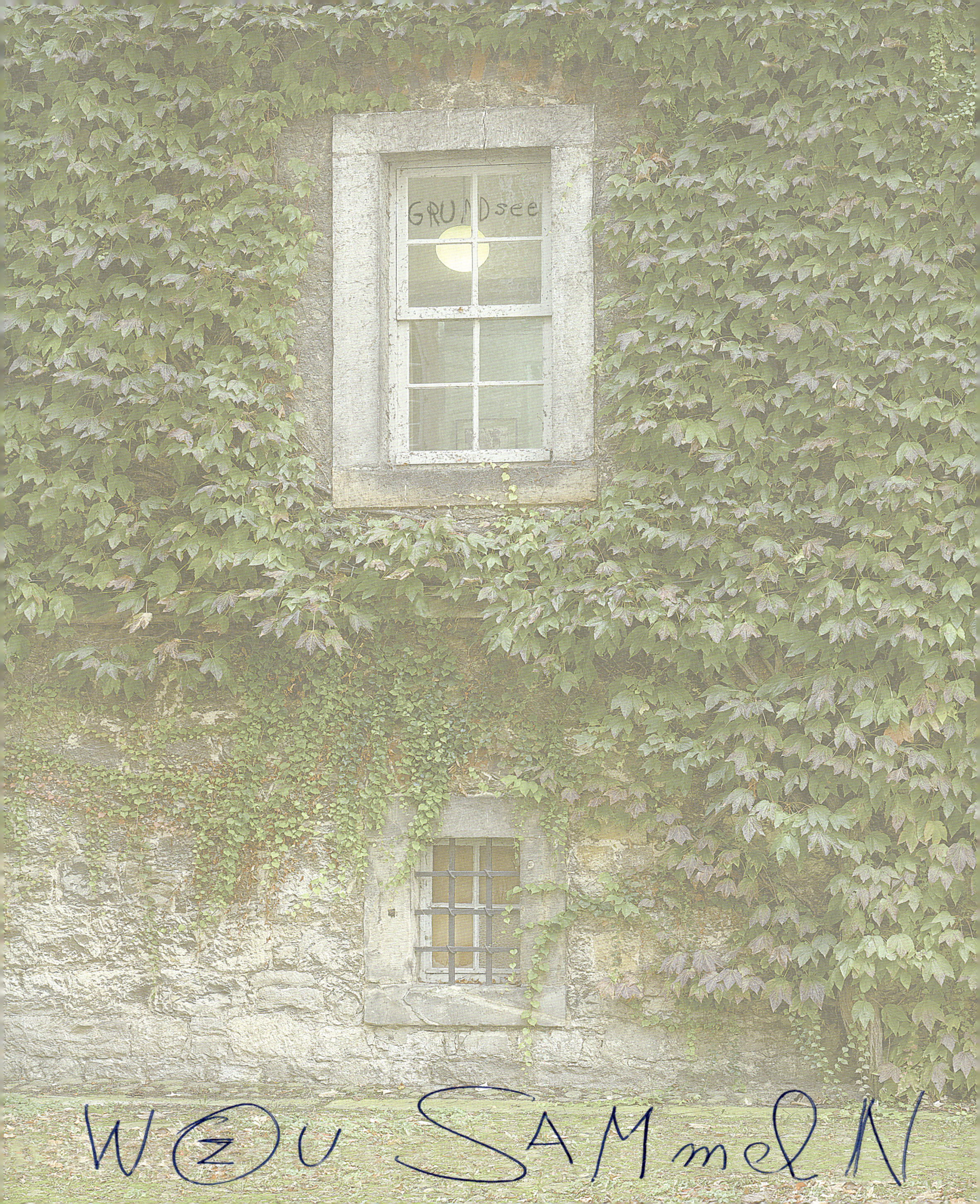
GRUNDsee
WZU SAMmelN

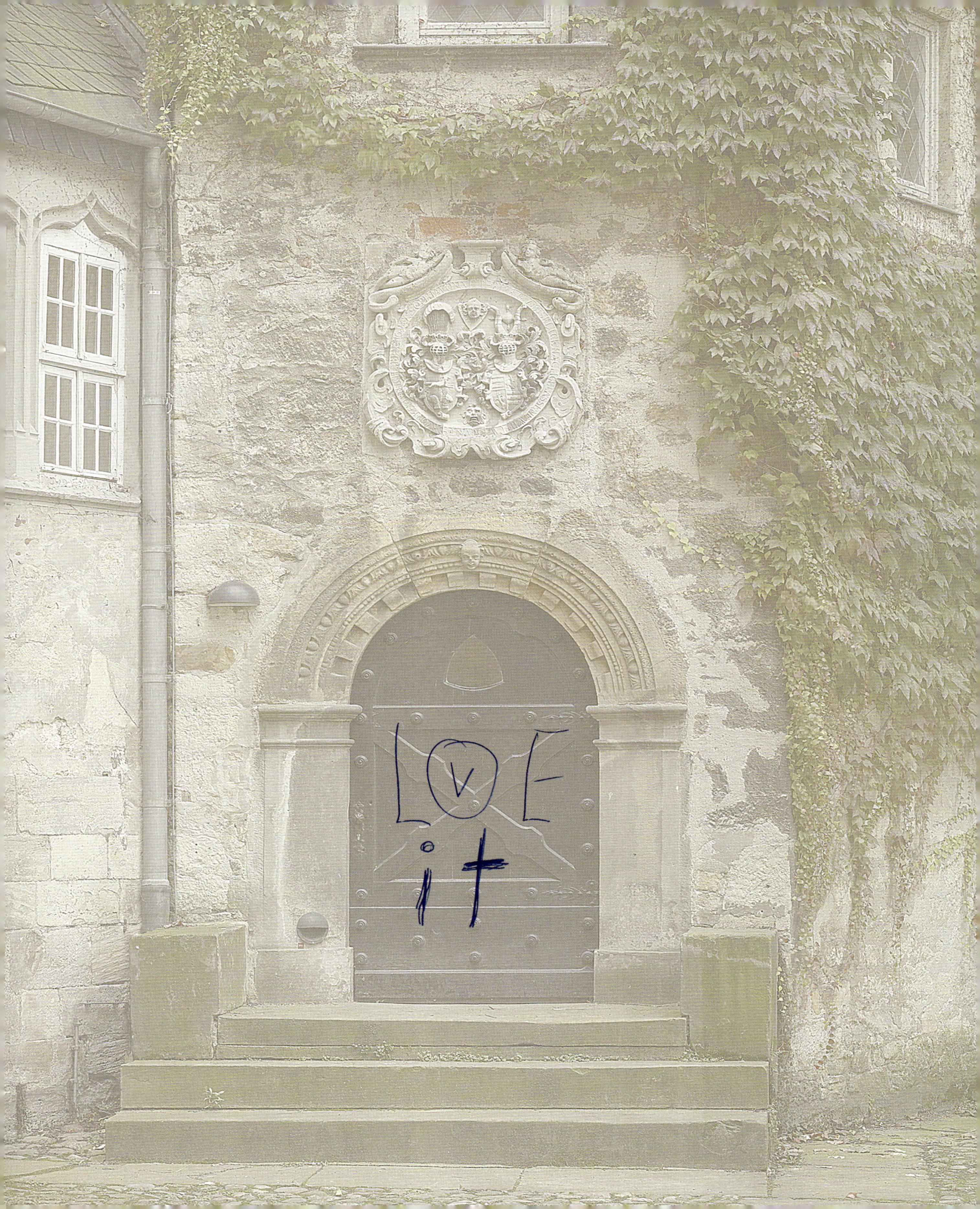
LOVE
it

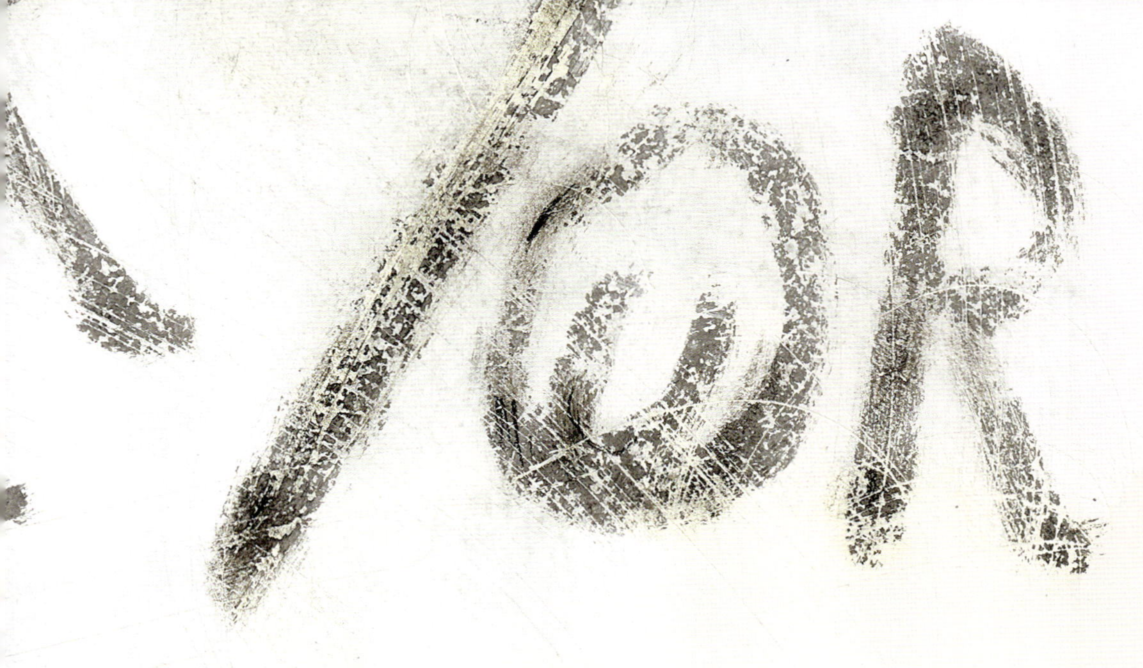

WERKE AUS DER SAMMLUNG IM DIALOG MIT WANDMALEREIEN VON ROLAND SCHAPPERT

FÜRS ALL GENUG

40 JAHRE STÄDTISCHE GALERIE WOLFSBURG
21. OKTOBER 2014 BIS 30. AUGUST 2015

ARTTermostat

DOES THE ARTIST TALK YOUR TALK

Susanne Pflegger

Beim Gang durch unsere Sammlungsausstellung „FÜRS ALL GENUG" erinnere ich mich an eine Kindergeschichte von Alberto Moravia. Sie spielt am Nordpol, wo es – wie der italienische Schriftsteller erzählt – vor einer Million Jahren viele hundert Grad kälter war als heute. „Bei einer solchen Kälte gefror alles", schreibt Moravia, „sogar, ihr werdet es nicht glauben, aber trotzdem ist es so, sogar die Gedanken. Sobald jemand dachte: ‚So eine Saukälte!', da bildete sich über seinem Kopf eine Art Dampfwölkchen und in dem Wölkchen stand in Eisbuchstaben zu lesen: ‚So eine Saukälte!' Die Tatsache der gefrorenen und somit sichtbaren Gedanken hatte schließlich zu dem logischen Ergebnis geführt, dass am Nordpol keiner mehr den Mut hatte, auch nur irgendetwas zu denken. Alle hatten Angst, die anderen könnten ihre Gedanken lesen. So kam es, dass die Eisbären, Pinguine, Seehunde, Schlittenhunde, Eskimos, alle nichts mehr dachten. Kurz, es war eine Welt von Dummköpfen, nicht weil sie unfähig gewesen wären zu denken; sondern aus Zartgefühl."*

Wie die gefrorenen Wolken in Moravias Erzählung wabern die Wandschriftbilder von Roland Schappert mit einzelnen Worten, Sätzen oder Wortkombinationen und Wortspielen durch die Ausstellungsräume. Wir haben den Kölner Künstler eingeladen, sich für die Präsentation einer neuen Dauerausstellung mit der Sammlung der Städtischen Galerie Wolfsburg auseinanderzusetzen und

Walking through our exhibition FÜRS ALL GENUG | ENOUGH FOR THE UNIVERSE featuring works from the museum collection, I am reminded of a children's story by Alberto Moravia. It takes place in the polar regions a million years ago, where, according to the Italian writer, the temperature could suddenly fall to a billion degrees below zero. "And when it was as cold as that, everything would freeze," writes Moravia, "even – you won't believe it, but it's true – even thoughts. As soon as anyone thought, for example 'It's so bitterly cold', then a little cloud of water vapour immediately formed over his or her head, and inside the little cloud, in letters of sharp ice and dripping like stalactites, you could read: 'It's so bitterly cold.' The fact that thoughts could freeze, and were consequently visible, led to the logical conclusion that nobody at the pole had the courage to think about anything. They were all afraid that the others could read their minds. So in the end polar bears, penguins, seals, huskies, Eskimos – everybody thought about nothing at all. It was, in short, a world of nincompoops. But they were nincompoops not so much because they were totally incapable of thinking, but rather out of politeness and the kindness of their hearts."*

In a similar way to the frozen clouds in Moravia's story, Roland Schappert's inscriptions on the walls comprising individual letters, sentences or combinations of words or puns float through the exhibition rooms. We invited the Cologne-based artist to take a close look at the Städtische Galerie Wolfsburg's collection in the run-up to the

im Dialog mit den Gemälden, Installationen, Videoprojektionen, der Skulptur sowie der Grafik eine Ausstellung mit „seinen" Gedanken zusammenzustellen. Das Ziel war, kritische Einblicke und frische Energien in der Rezeption freizulegen. Auf das von Moravia beschriebene „Zartgefühl" musste hier keine Rücksicht genommen werden, ganz im Gegenteil: Neue Zusammenhänge und provokante Fragen waren erwünscht.

Unsere Sammlungsausstellungen zeitgenössischer Kunst werden im Westflügel von Schloss Wolfsburg präsentiert, der Mitte des 19. Jahrhunderts errichtet wurde. Auf zwei Etagen kann jeweils nur eine Auswahl des Sammlungsbestands gezeigt werden. Die Räume sind kleinteilig und dienten den Grafen von der Schulenburg bis 1942 als Wohn- und Schlafgemächer. Ein besonderer Ort ist die im Nordflügel anschließende „Silberkammer", die ins 14. Jahrhundert datiert wird. Sie ist heute der Schwarzraum, die „black box". Durch die Überführung der Ausstellungen in die Räume eines Schlosses, das Heim und Repräsentationsort einer Familie war, entsteht eine ganz bestimmte Situation: Da der Westflügel keinen neutralen Ausstellungsraum darstellt, sondern deutlich Geschichte und Geschichten in die zeitgenössischen Exponate einschreibt, stellt sich zwangsläufig die Frage, wie das Zeigen in diesem Kontext funktioniert. Schappert thematisiert in der Ausstellung „FÜRS ALL GENUG" Aspekte des Sammelns und stellt gleichzeitig Fragen an die museale Präsentation. Die Text-Bild-Installationen schaffen komplexe Räume, die das „Zeigen des Zeigens", wie Bazon Brock definiert, kritisch

presentation of a new permanent exhibition and to compile his own exhibition with "his" thoughts in a dialogue with the paintings, installations, video projections, sculpture and print graphics. The overall aim was to generate a critical insight into and fresh energy for the reception of the collection. However, in this instance it was not necessary to take account of the "kindness" Moravia describes, on the contrary: new connections and provocative questions were positively called for.

Our exhibitions featuring the museum's contemporary art collection are held in the west wing of Schloss Wolfsburg, which was built in the middle of the nineteenth century. Presentations of this kind across two storeys understandably only allow for a section of the overall collection to be shown. The rooms themselves are small and once served the aristocratic von der Schulenburg family until 1942 as living quarters and bedchambers. The so-called adjacent "silver chamber", situated in the north wing and dating back to the fourteenth century, is a place of particular interest. Today, it constitutes the "black box". A special situation has been created by transferring the exhibition into the rooms of the palace, once the home and representational locus of a family: because the west wing is not a neutral exhibition space as such, but is clearly inscribed with history and the stories behind the contemporary exhibits, this naturally gives rise to the question of how exhibiting itself functions in this context. Schappert focuses thematically in the exhibition FÜRS ALL GENUG | ENOUGH FOR THE UNIVERSE upon aspects of collecting and, at the same time, poses questions relating to its presentation in a museum context. The combined textual and visual installations give rise to com-

kommentieren, aber auch mit einem Augenzwinkern humorvoll persiflieren. Die Ausstellung wird zu einem eigenen Medium, ein offener Prozess, der vielfältige Aussagen zulässt. ZEITGEIST WANDERT WEITER.

Die Möglichkeiten, was und vor allem wie Bilder zeigen können, werden von Roland Schappert dabei kreativ ausgelotet. Der Betrachter ist nicht nur direkt eingebunden in Gegenüberstellungen und Überlagerungen, sondern es entwickelt sich darüber hinaus ein subtiles System von Interaktionen zwischen Werk, Künstler und Rezipient. Die Schriftbilder machen dem Betrachter ein Angebot, mit den Exponaten in Beziehung zu treten, mit ihnen umzugehen oder sie auf eine bestimmte Weise zu betrachten. Sie legen aber nichts fest und bleiben aufgrund der von Schappert gewählten sprachlichen Formulierungen und ihrer visuellen Erscheinung mehrdeutig.

Es wird nicht bestimmt, was man zu sehen hat, vielmehr entscheidet der Betrachter mit dem, was er an Assoziationsbereitschaft und Abstraktionsvermögen mitbringt, selbst über das, was ihm die Bilder zeigen können. So entwickelt sich ein Kontext, der über das Sehen hinausgeht. DOES THE ARTIST TALK YOUR TALK? Im Leitbild der Städtischen Galerie haben wir verankert, dass die Kompetenz und das soziale Eingebundensein unserer Besucherinnen und Besucher ebenso wie ihre Unterschiedlichkeit in Bezug auf Alter, Herkunft, Motivation, Interesse und Wissen akzeptiert und beherzigt werden. Unser Ziel ist es, Freiräume und offene Situationen zu erzeugen, die eigene Erfahrun-

plex spaces which comment critically upon the art of "exhibiting the exhibition", to coin Bazon Brock's definition, but also adopting a satirical, humorous, tongue-in-cheek approach. The exhibition becomes its own medium, an open process permitting an array of diverse messages. AND THE ZEITGEIST GOES ON.

At the same time, Roland Schappert creatively explores the possibilities of what and, primarily, how paintings can show things. Not only is the viewer directly incorporated into the juxtapositions and superimpositions, but, over and above that, a subtle system of interaction between the works, the artist and the recipient also begins to unfold. The inscriptions on the walls offer the viewer an opportunity to connect with the exhibits, a possible approach to them or a particular way of viewing them. However, far from fixing a given interpretation, they remain open and equivocal as a result of Schappert's chosen wordings and their visual presentation.

At no point is there a determination about what should or shouldn't be seen, rather the viewer determines his readiness to make associations and draws on his ability to make abstractions about whatever the paintings themselves might show. Thus, a context is generated that extends beyond mere seeing. DOES THE ARTIST TALK YOUR TALK? Our model for the Städtische Galerie is intended to accommodate the competence and social inclusivity of our audience, as well as accepting and paying heed to this audience's diversity in terms of age, origin, motivation, interest and knowledge. Our aim is to create both scope and open, flexible situations that enable visitors to generate personal experience from their engagement with the various artworks in the col-

gen möglich machen. Das Museum und seine Sammlung sollen die Lust am Entdecken wecken. Neugierde und die Fähigkeit zur visuellen Erkenntnis können durch die Auseinandersetzung mit den Originalen gefördert werden. Kein vorgeschriebener Ausstellungsrundgang mit gesetzter Deutung also, vielmehr Freude, Subjektivität, Intuition. Ich danke Roland Schappert, dass er sich mit uns auf das Wagnis dieser Sammlungsinszenierung mit eigenständigem Werkcharakter eingelassen hat. Der Künstler war hier Produzent, Theoretiker und Kunstkritiker in einer Person.

Die Bewohner des Nordpols in Alberto Moravias Geschichte hören eines Tages von einem Land, wo es unheimlich warm sein soll. Dort im Tropenland gefrieren die Gedanken nicht. Es macht Spaß, ganz frei und ohne Angst zu denken …

*Zitiert nach: Alberto Moravia, „Als die Gedanken in der Luft gefroren", in: Wie der Hund und der Mensch Freunde wurden. Italienische Kindergeschichten, ausgewählt von Klaus Wagenbach, Berlin 1999, S.24–32 (S. 24).

lection. The museum and its collection are likewise intended to awaken the joy of discovery. Curiosity and the ability to recognise and understand things can be furthered through visual experience via the engagement with original works. Consequently, in place of a set route through the exhibition with a preordained interpretation, there is subjectivity, delight and intuition. I should like to thank Roland Schappert for joining us in such an ambitious venture that this staging of the collection – effectively as a work in its own right – undoubtedly represents. The artist was producer, theorist and art critic all rolled into one.

One day, the denizens of the polar regions in Alberto Moravia's story hear about another country where it is supposed to be incredibly warm. Down in the tropics people's thoughts don't freeze. It's fun to be able to think freely and fearlessly …

*Quoted from: Alberto Moravia, "Quando i pensieri gelavano nell'aria" (When thoughts turn to ice), in: Storie della Preistoria, illustrated by Flaminia Siciliano, Milan: Bompiani, 1994, pp. 35–41 (p. 35), translation courtesy of Christina Coster-Longman, Florence.

Auf den Künstler Denkmalschutz!

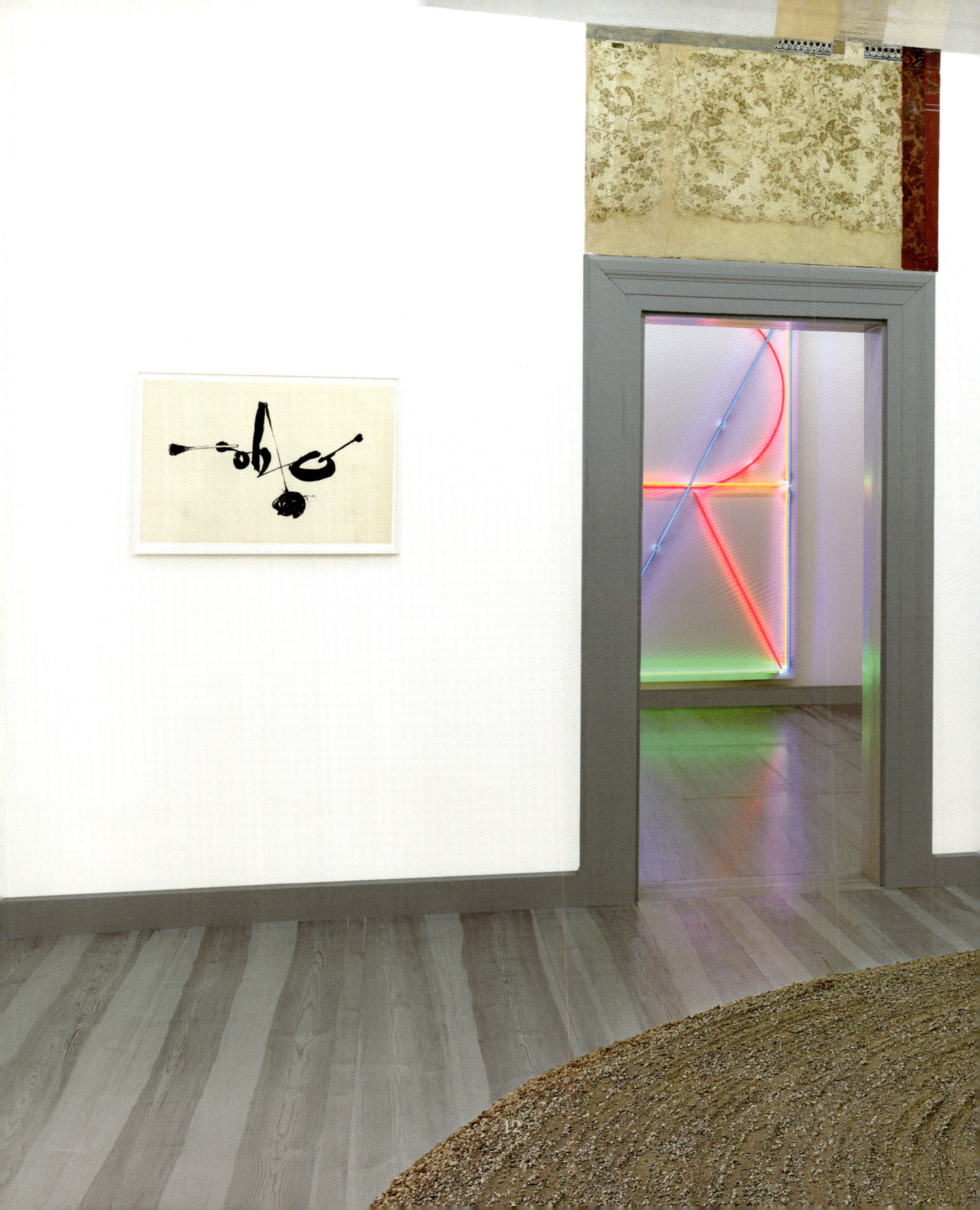

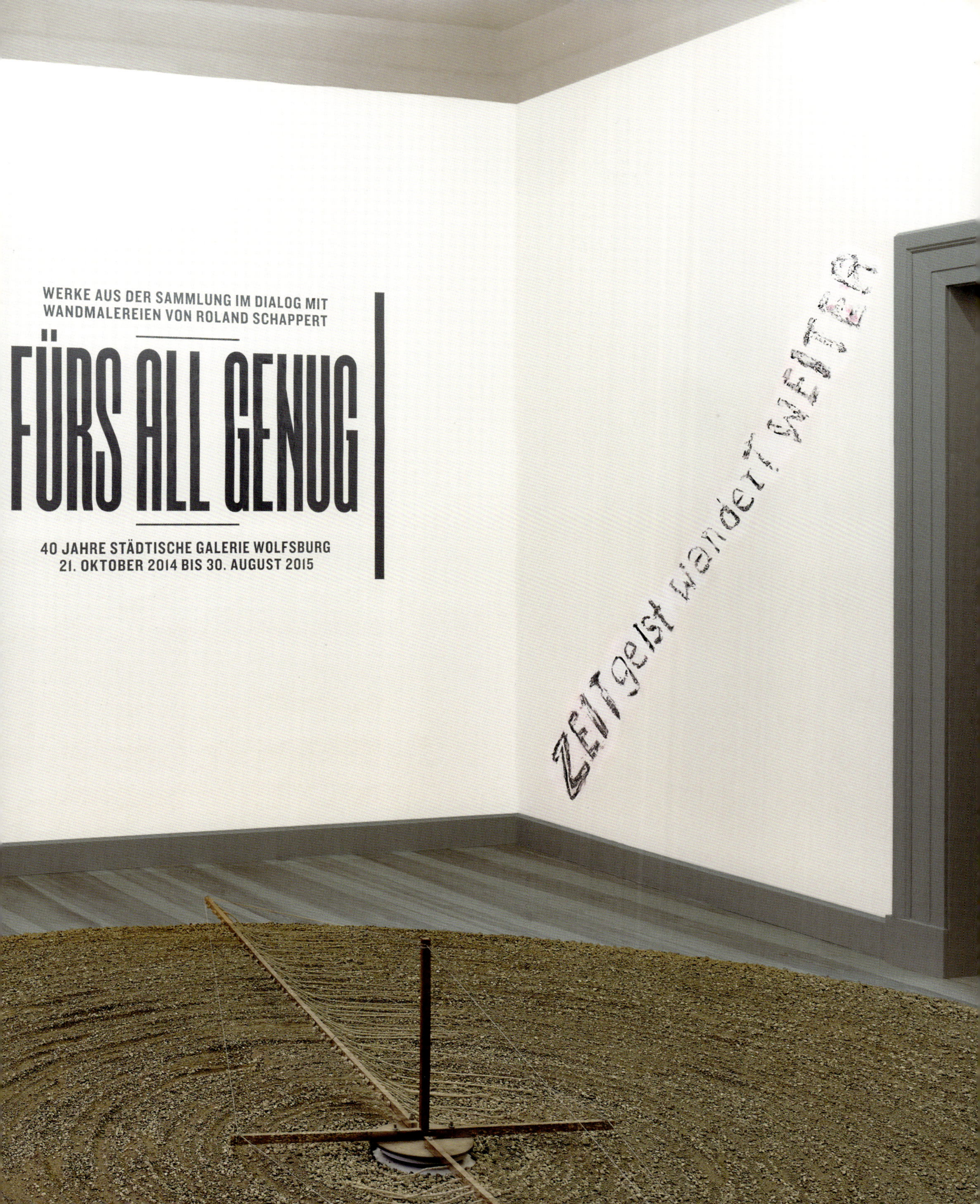
WERKE AUS DER SAMMLUNG IM DIALOG MIT
WANDMALEREIEN VON ROLAND SCHAPPERT
FÜRS ALL GENUG
40 JAHRE STÄDTISCHE GALERIE WOLFSBURG
21. OKTOBER 2014 BIS 30. AUGUST 2015
ZEITgeist wandert WEITER

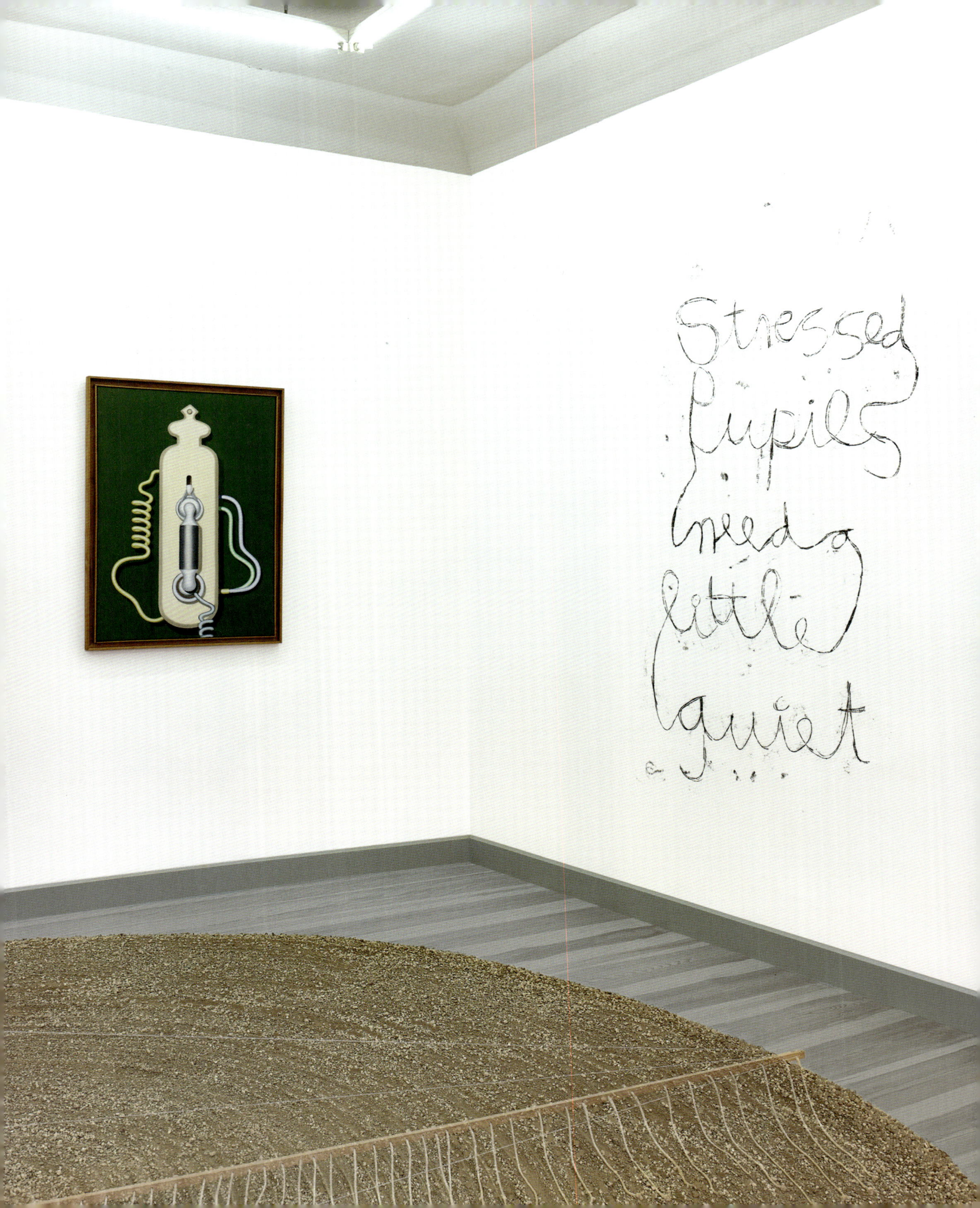
Stressed
Pupils
need a
little
quiet

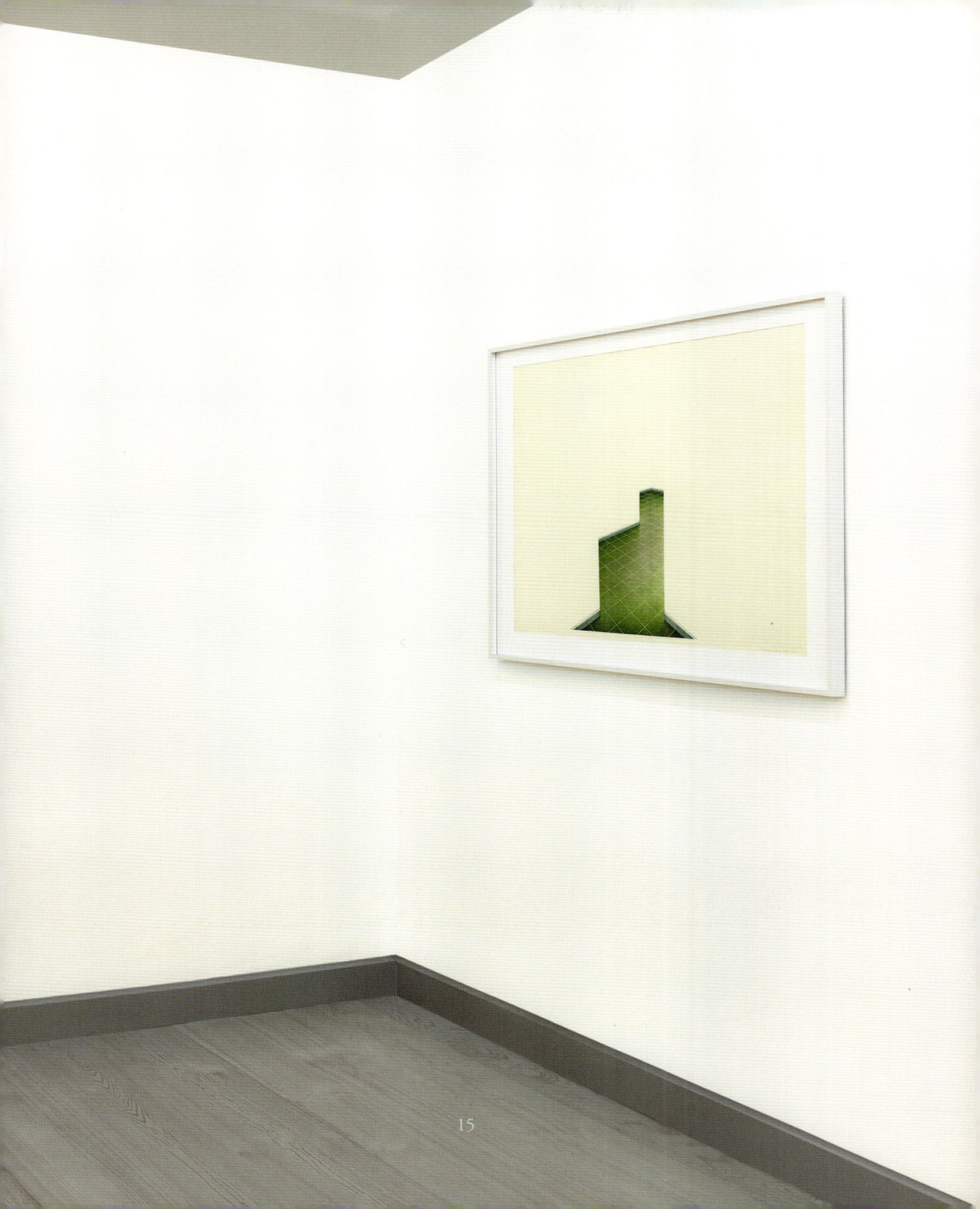

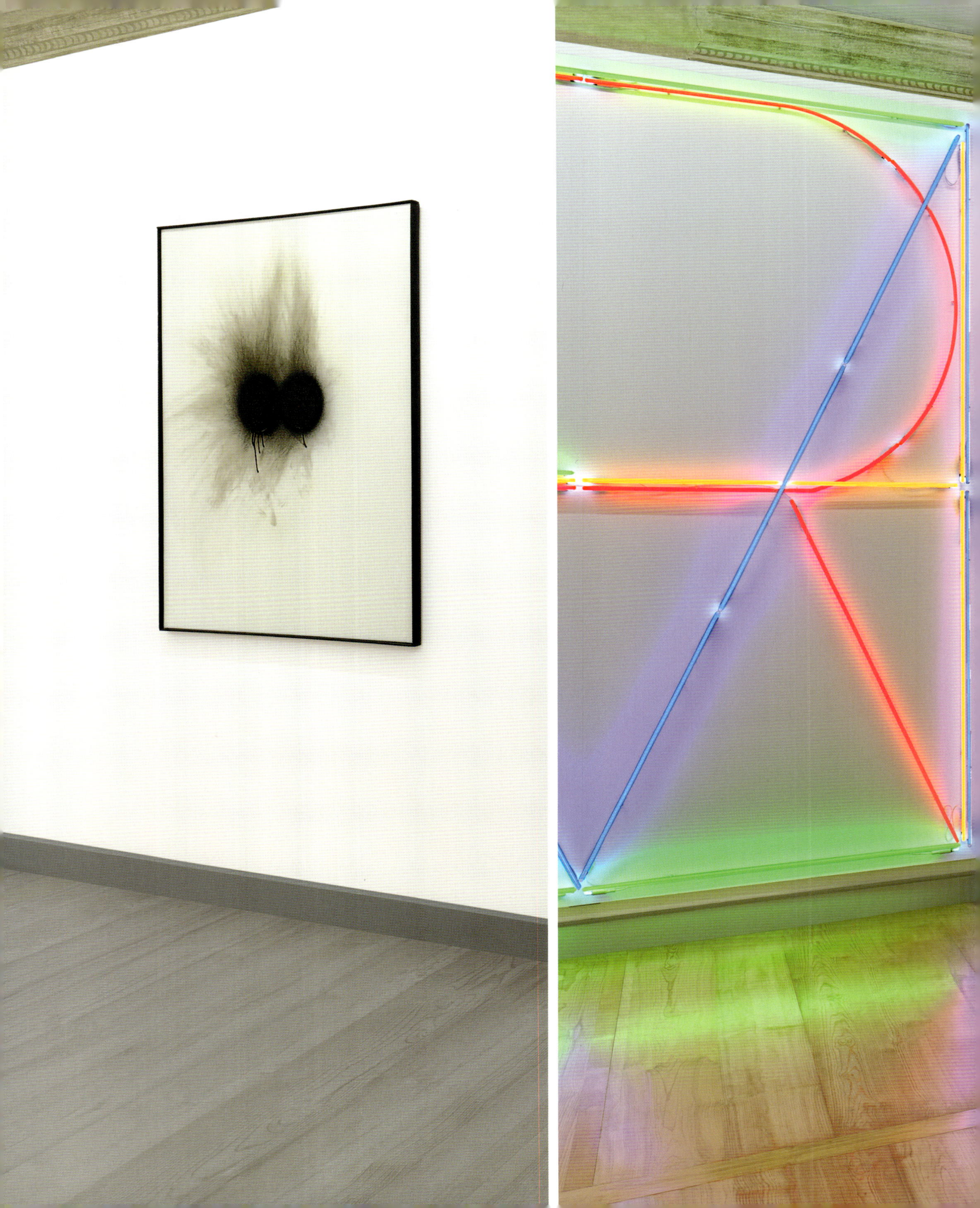

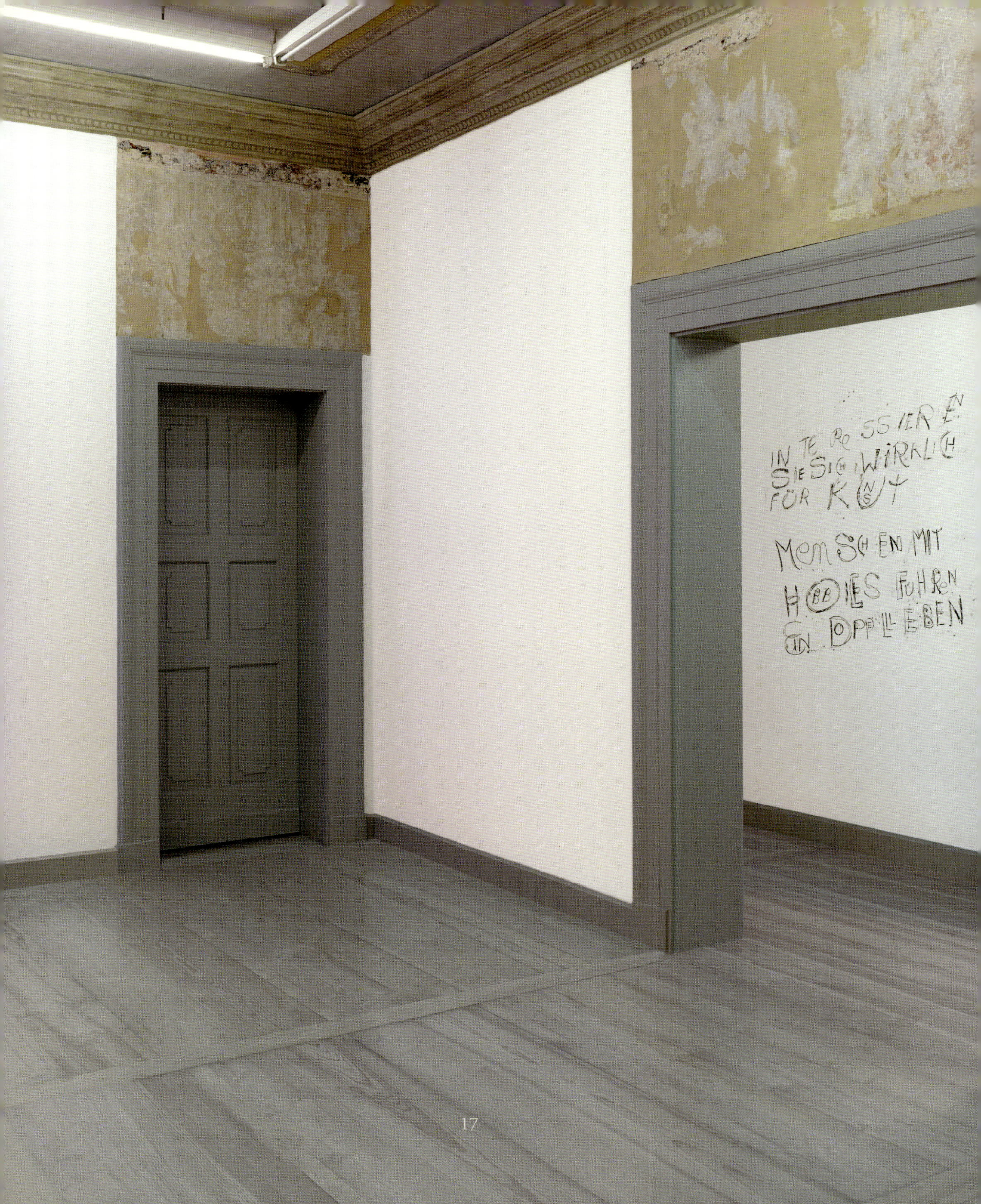

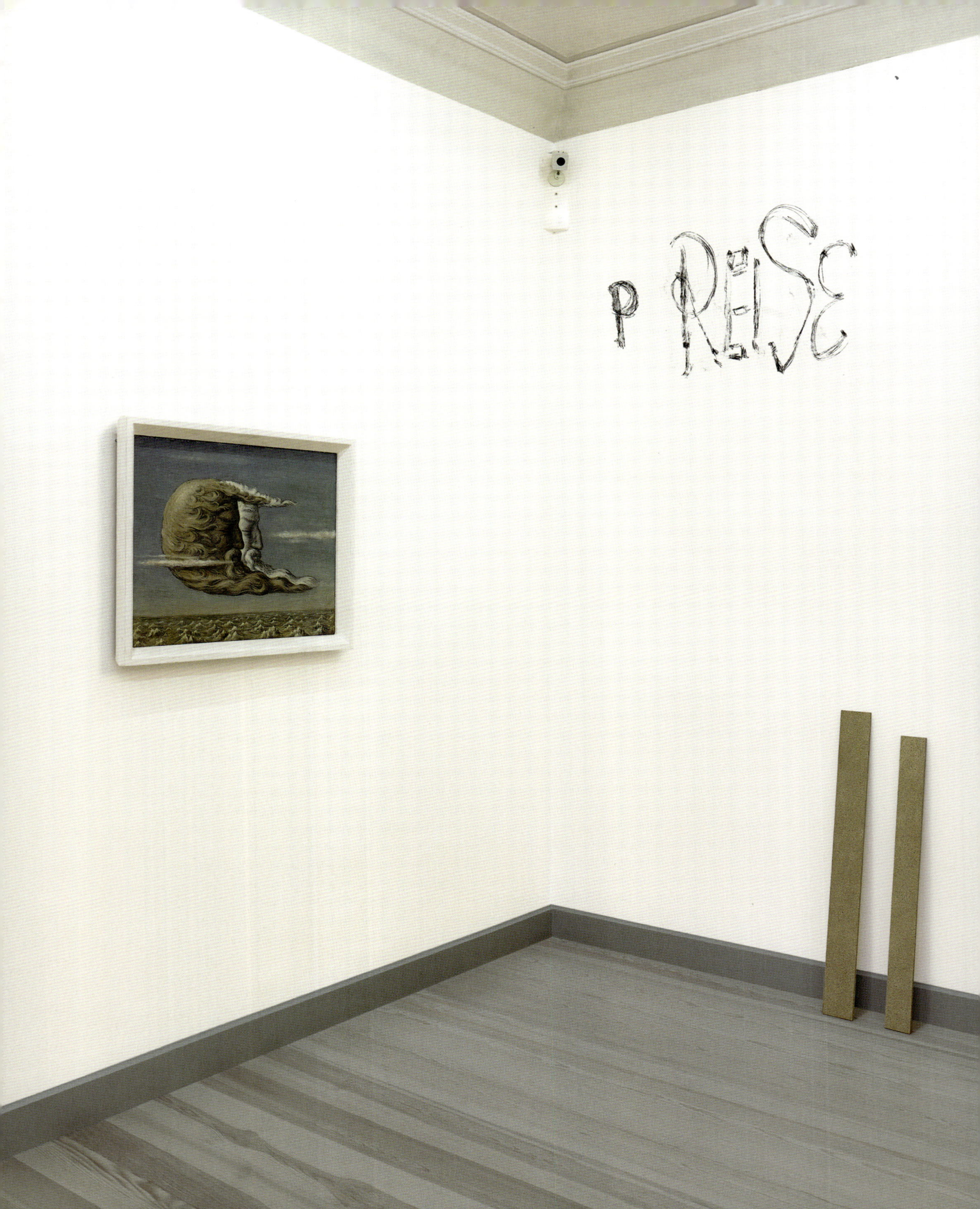

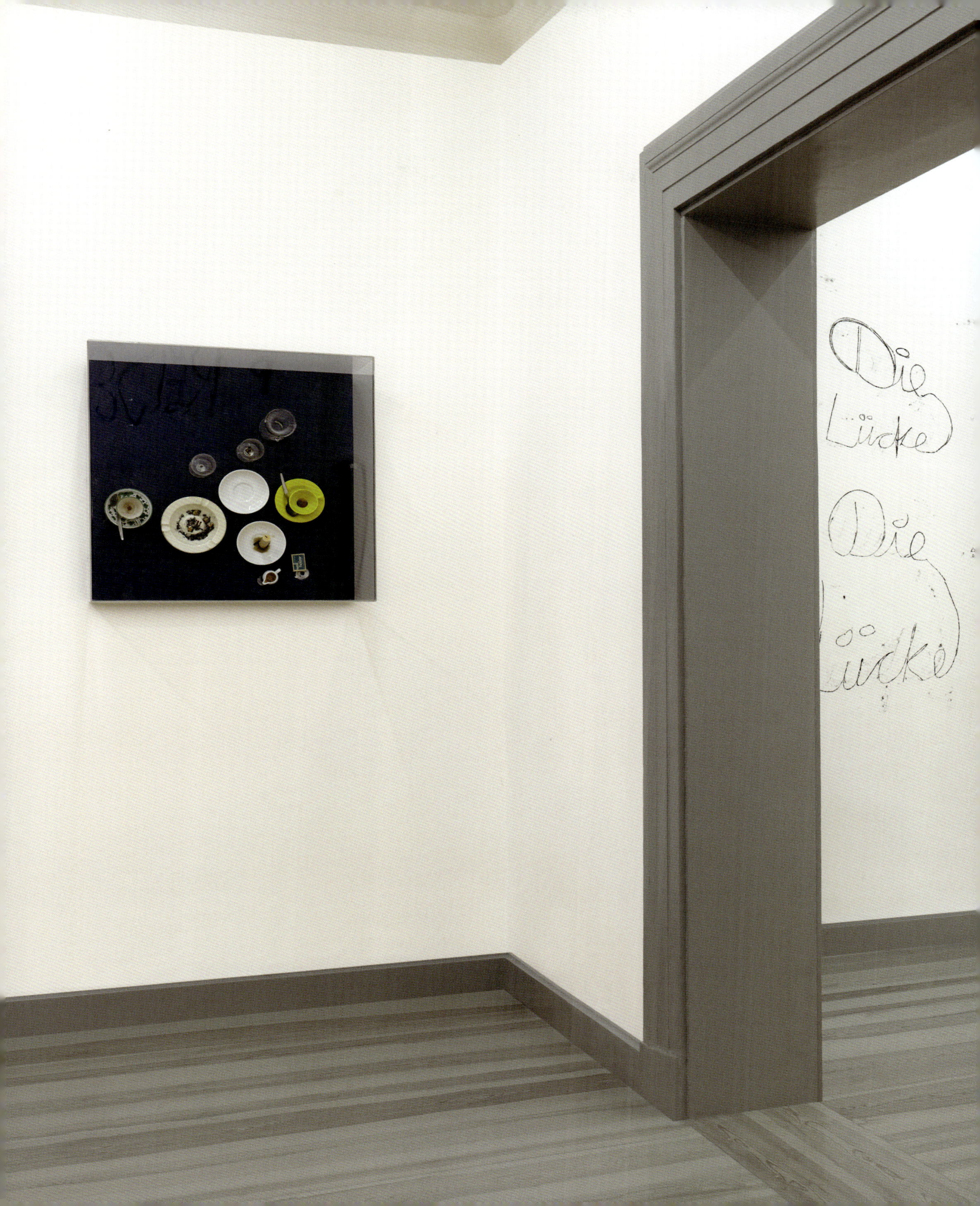
Die
Lücke
Die
Lücke

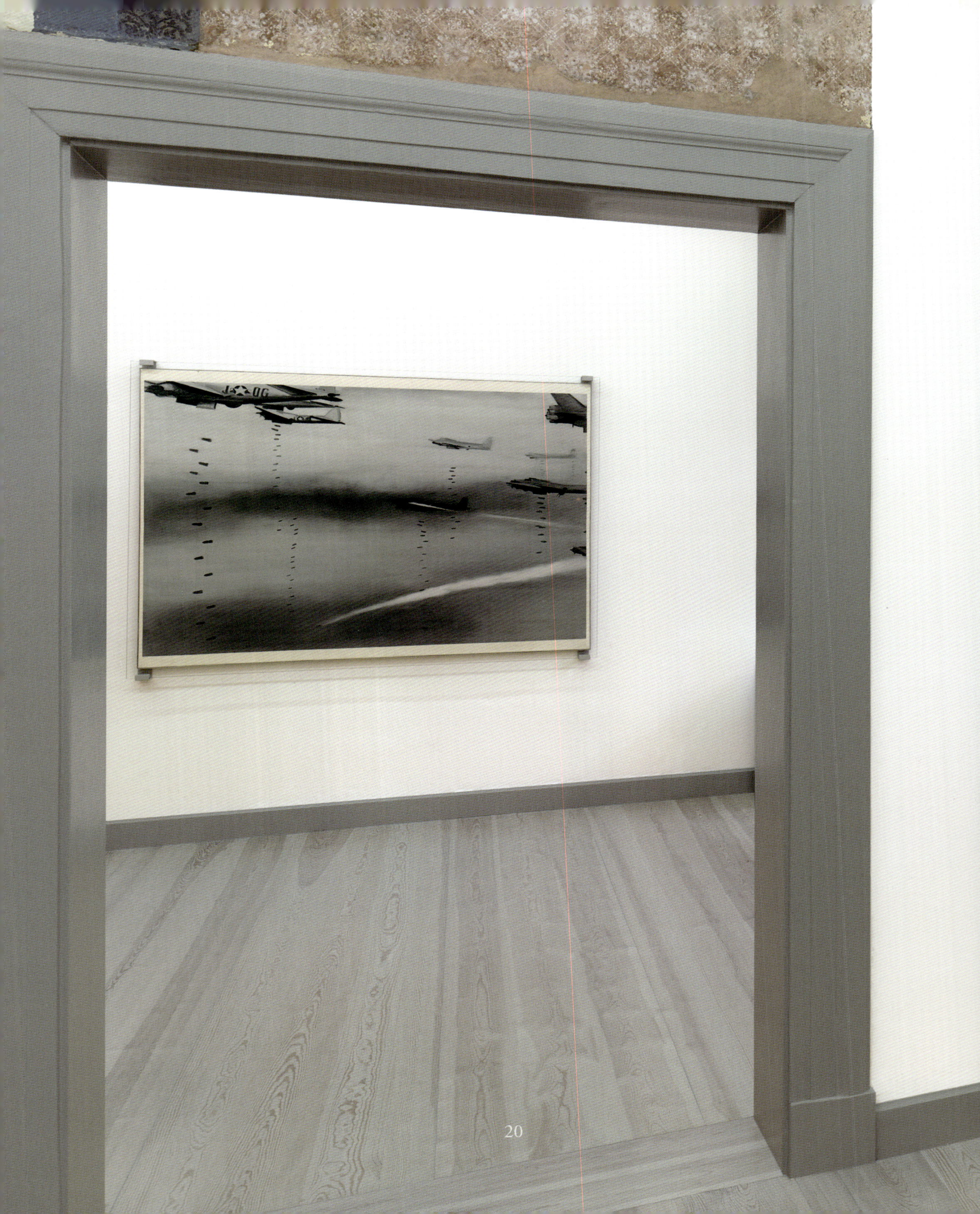

Die
Lücke

Die
Lücke

Die
Lücke

IV

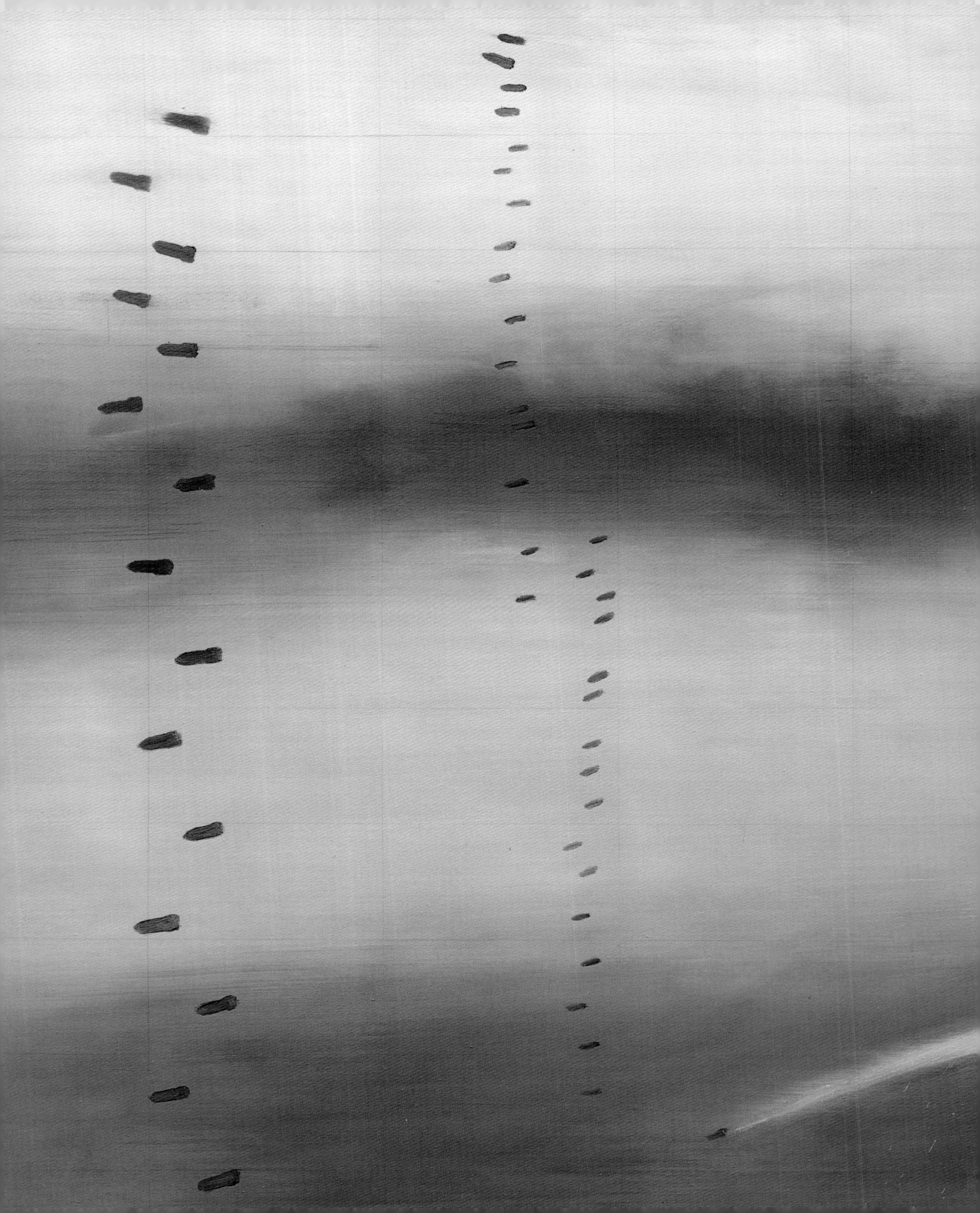

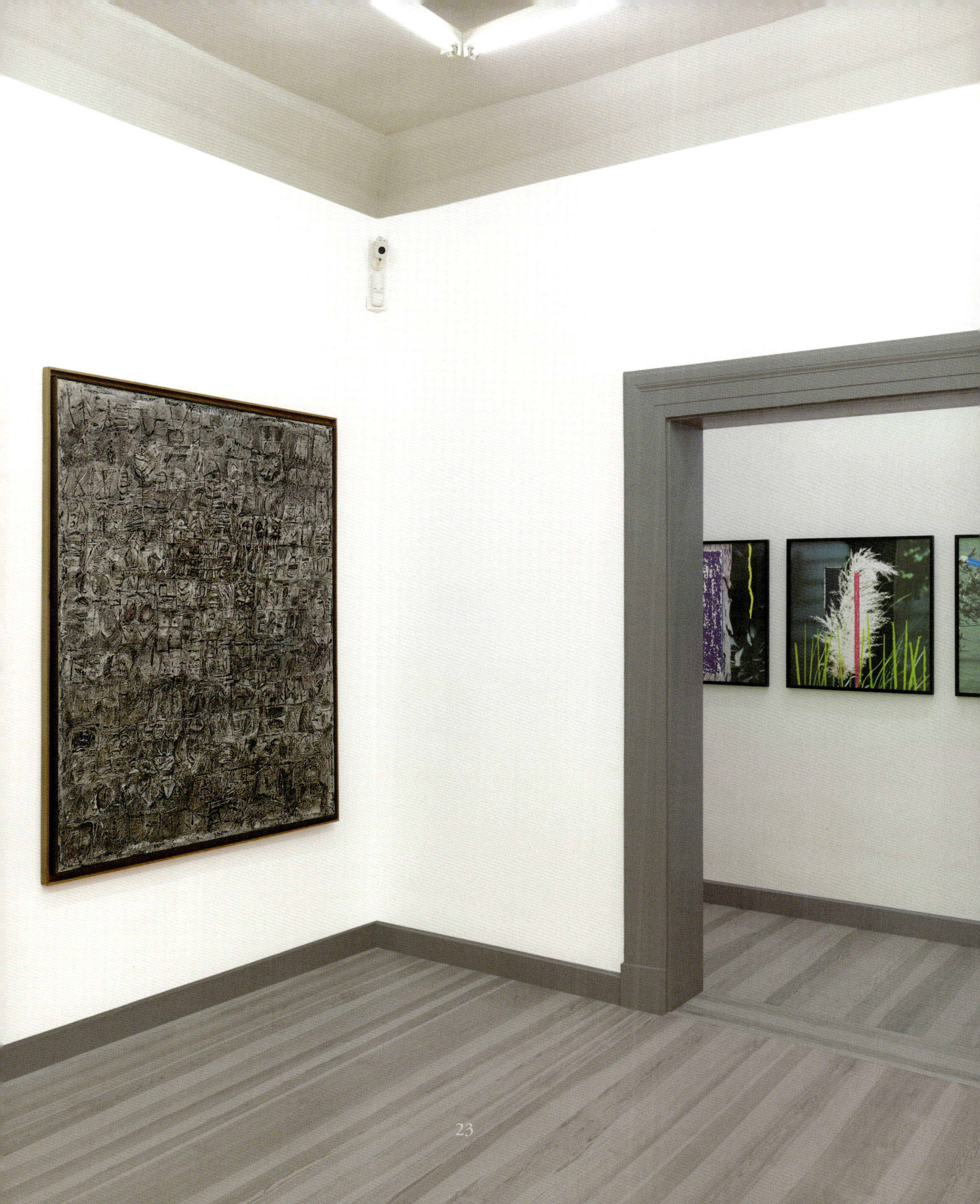

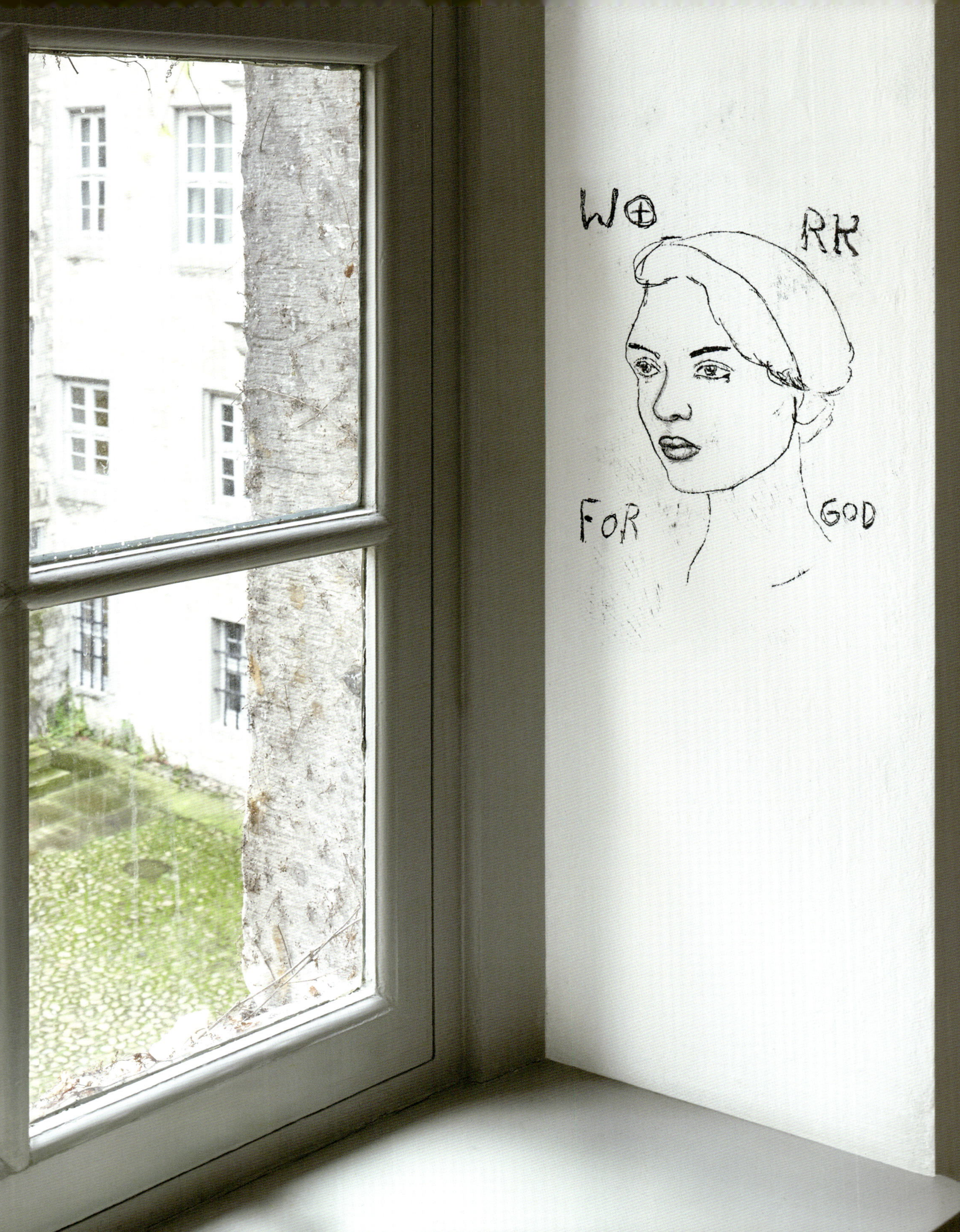
WO RK
FOR GOD

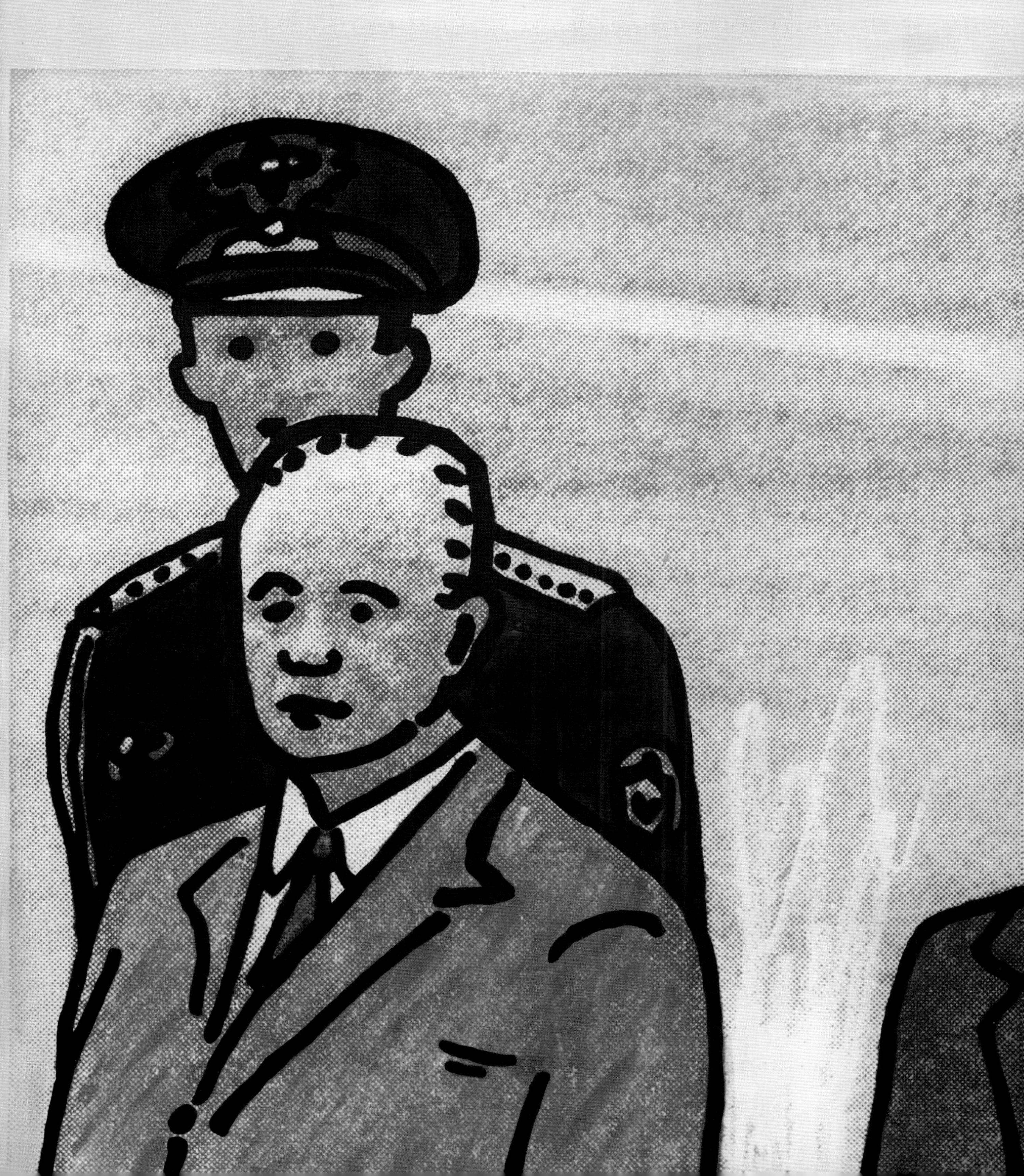

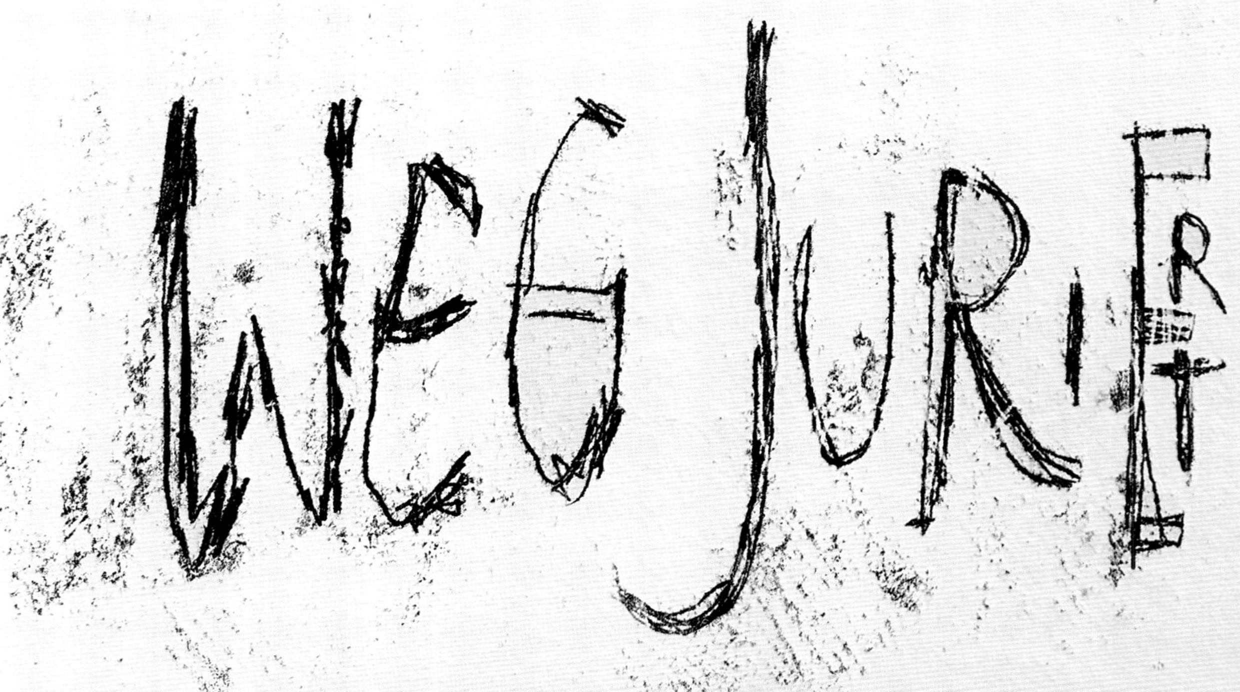

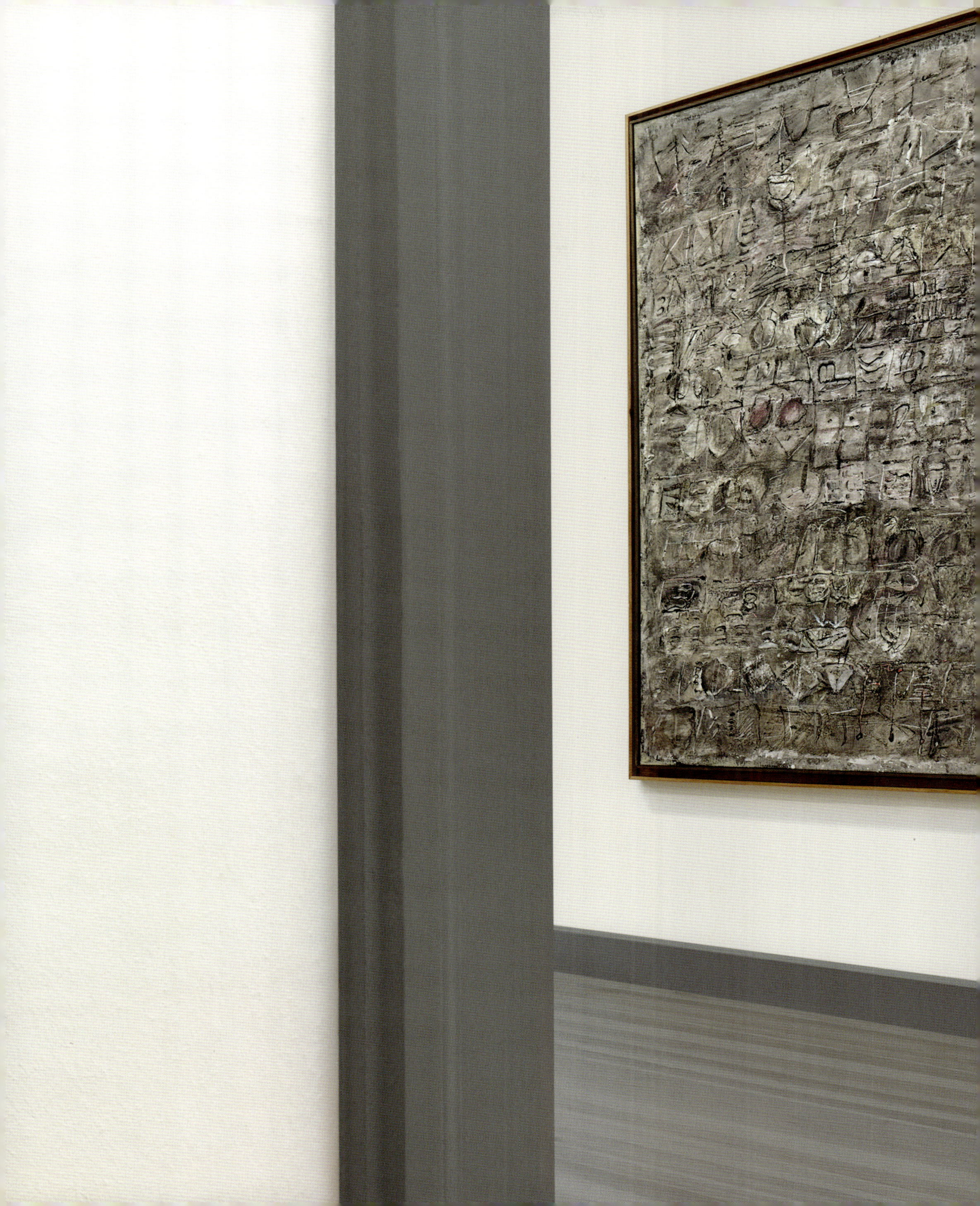

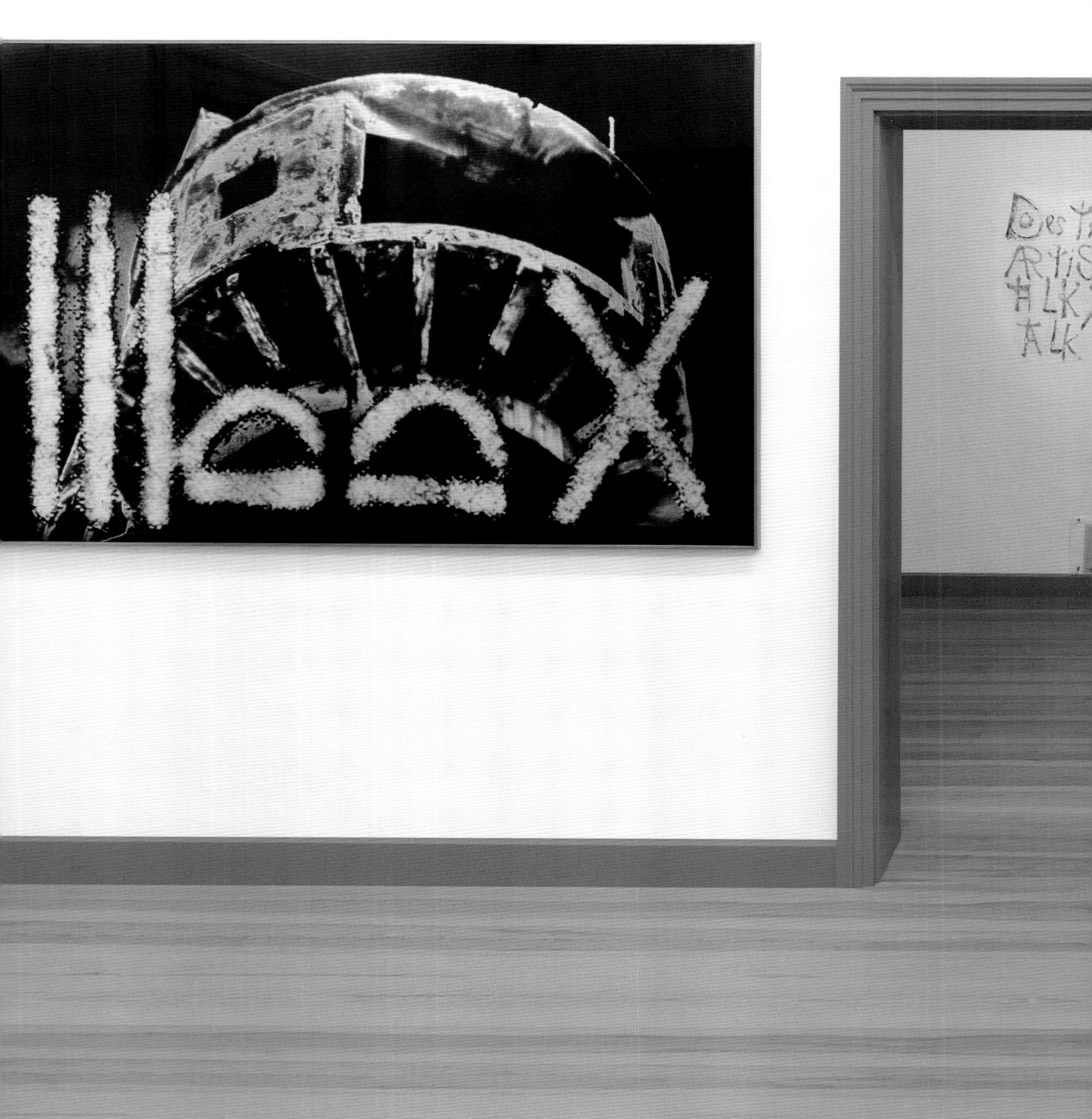

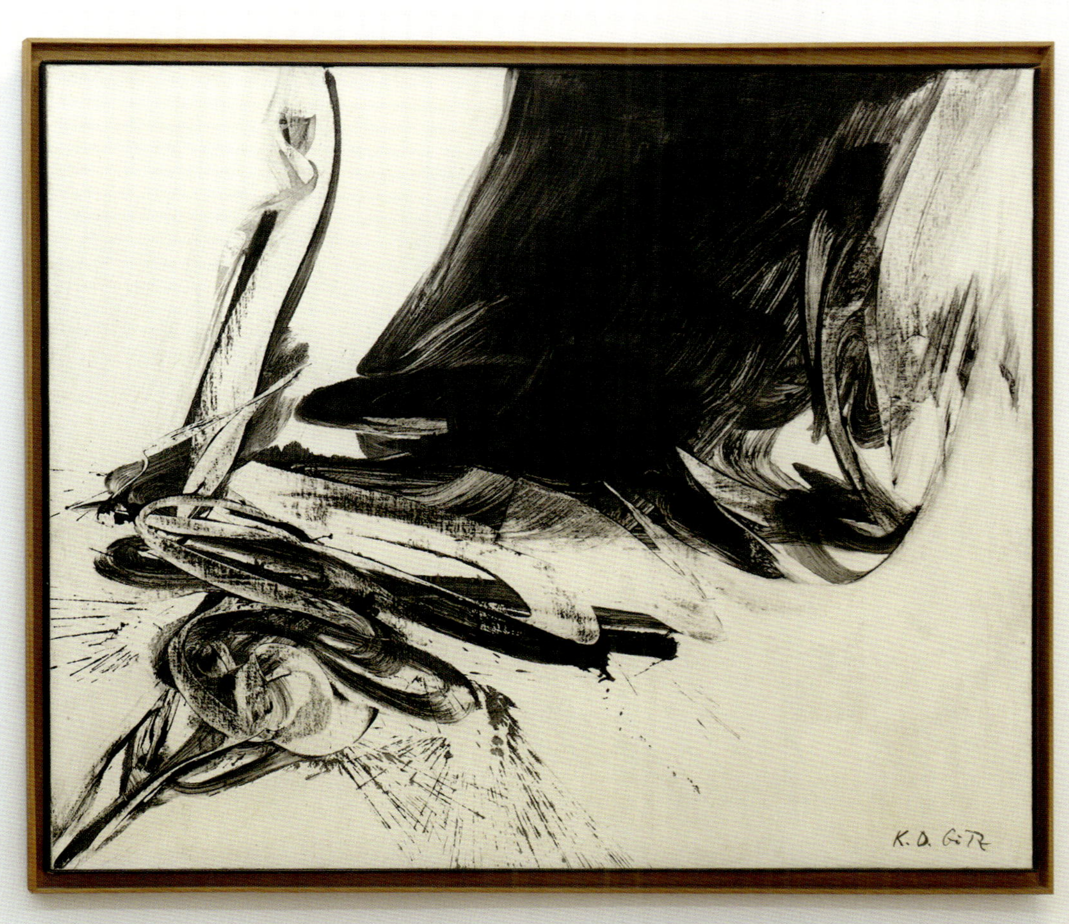

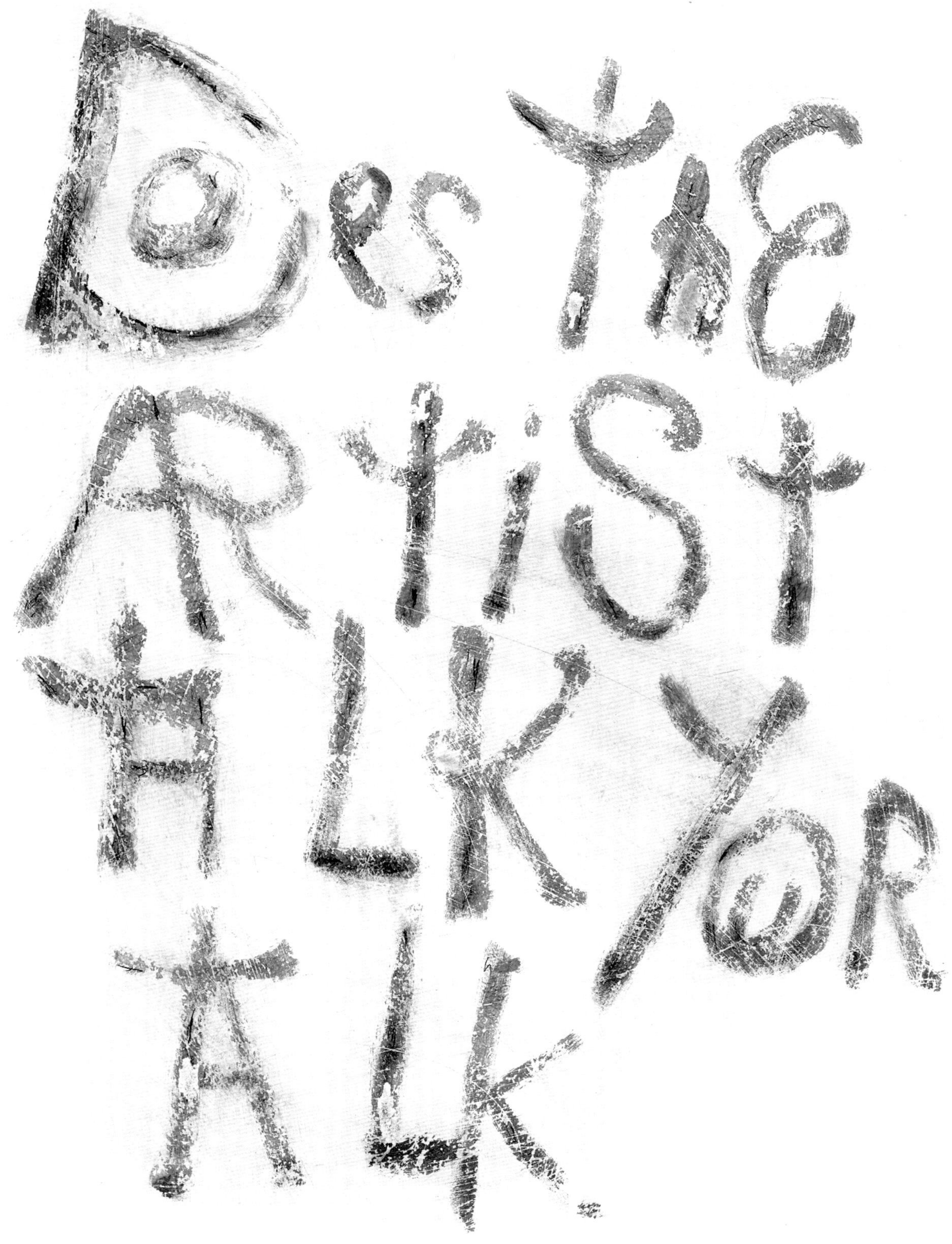
DOES THE
ARTIST
TALK YOUR
TALK

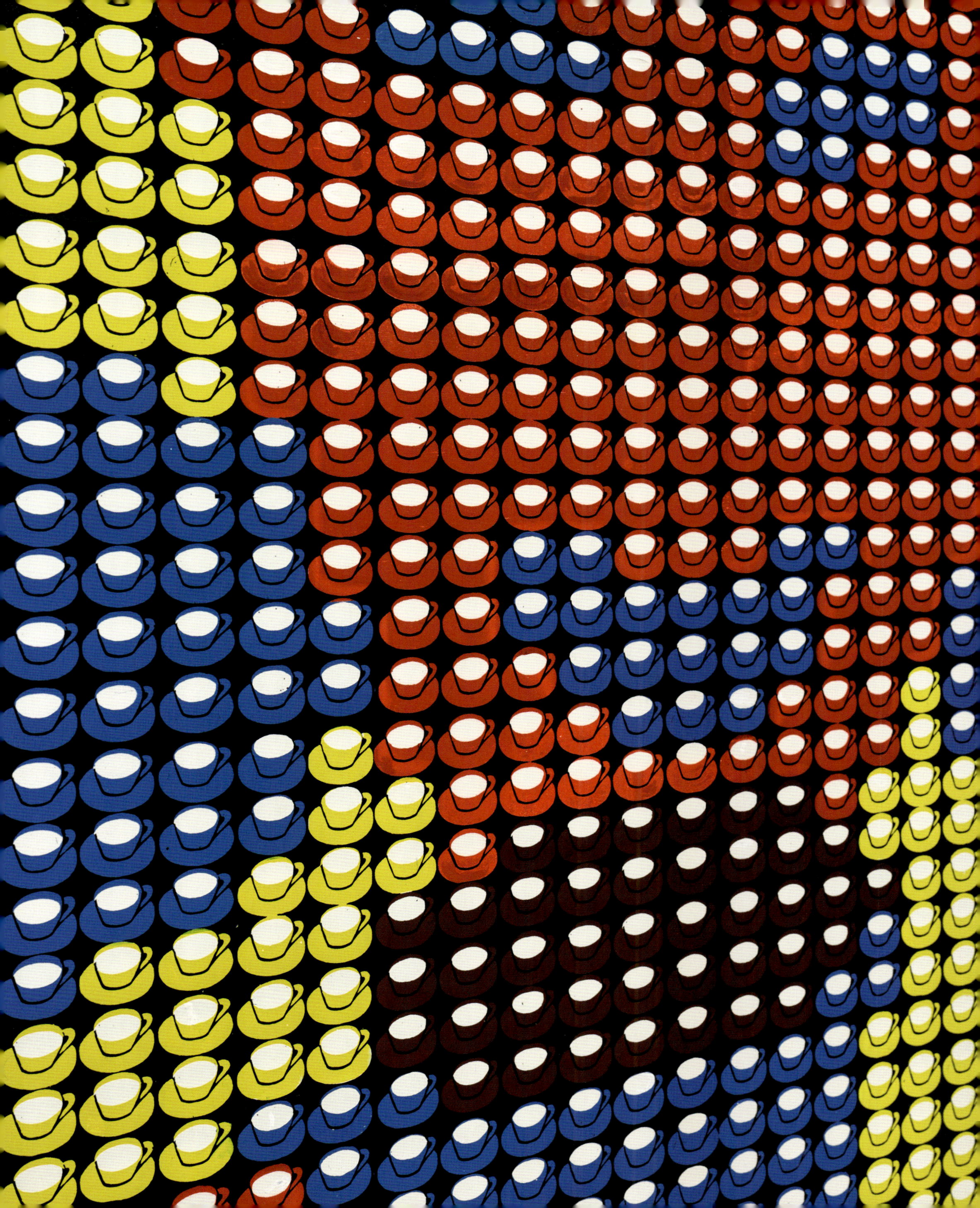

Everything I do is Wrong

Everything I do is wrong everything I do is Wrong

Wrong Wrong

Everything I do is ~~Wrong~~

Everything I do is Wrong. Everything I do is wrong

2 1/4

2 1/4 x 5 3/4

Out

Good

meo7.jpg djld01.jpg

ad1.jpg

(maybe) sweet01.jpg? shehe.jpg

biker127.jpg

biker 128.jpg

biker132.jpg

biker 133, 34-47!.jpg

dessert/ ~~mtg~~

/mtngtool.html

http://www.dm.de/

SONDERN + DAUER IV

KÜNSTLer scherT AUS

HÜbsch aBER UTOPIE

UN VOR SEH BAR

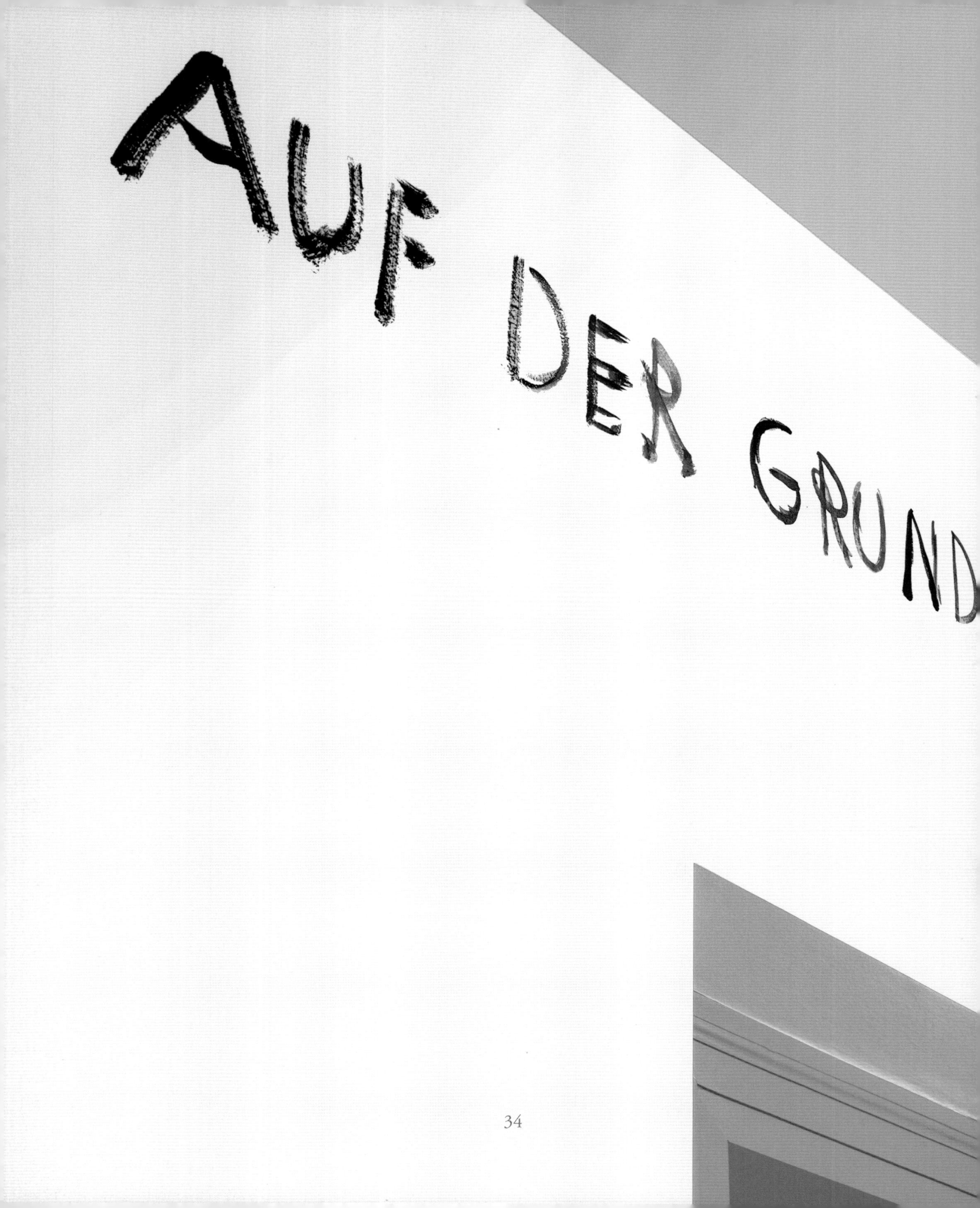

AUF DER GRUND

SORRY

FÜR ABHANDEN GEKOMMENE
GEGENSTÄNDE ÜBERNIMMT
DIE STADT WOLFSBURG KEINE
HAFTUNG

KLEINEIDEEN KRISE

EIN AUSGANG

RASCH SCHWANKENDER WERTVORSTELLUNGEN

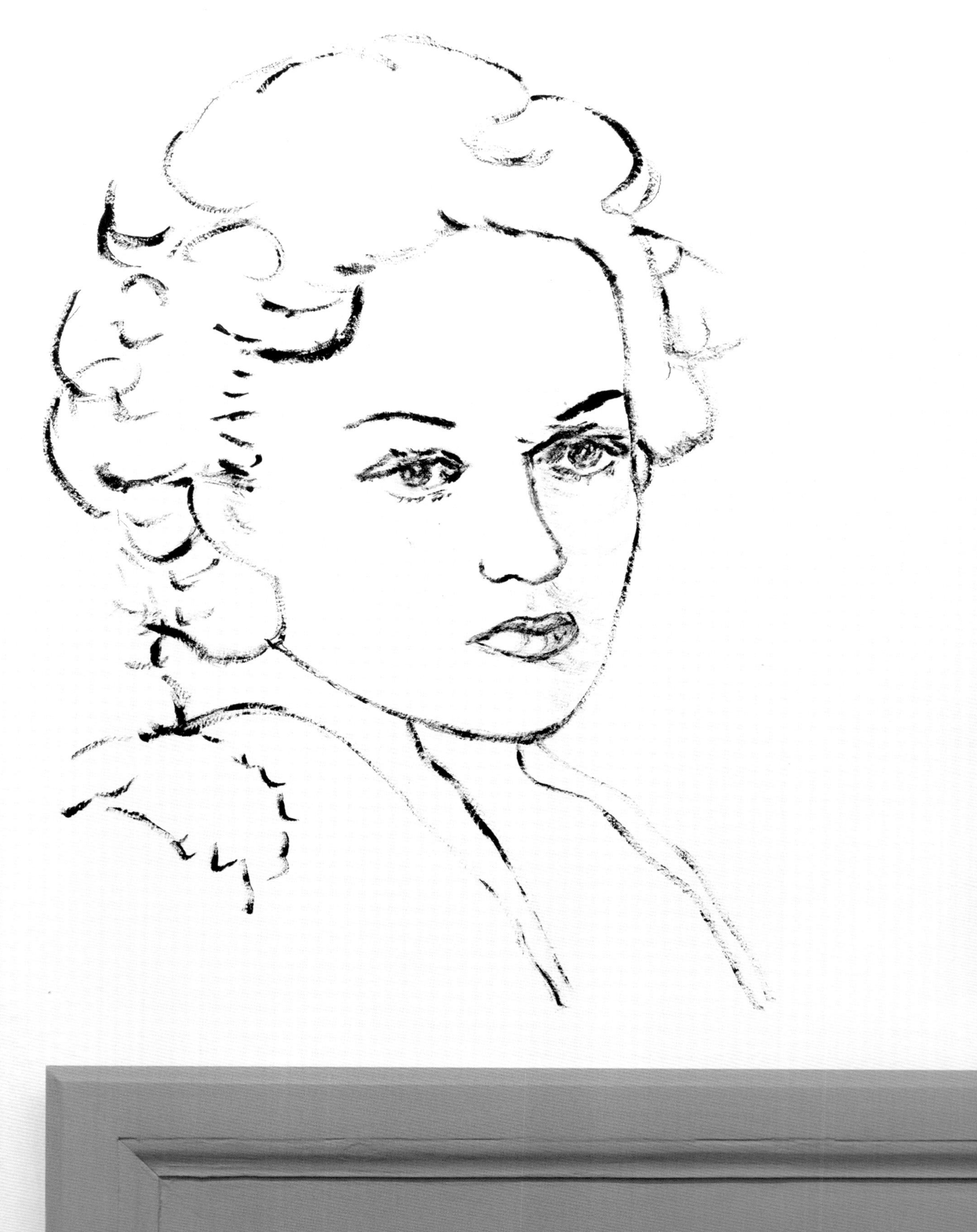

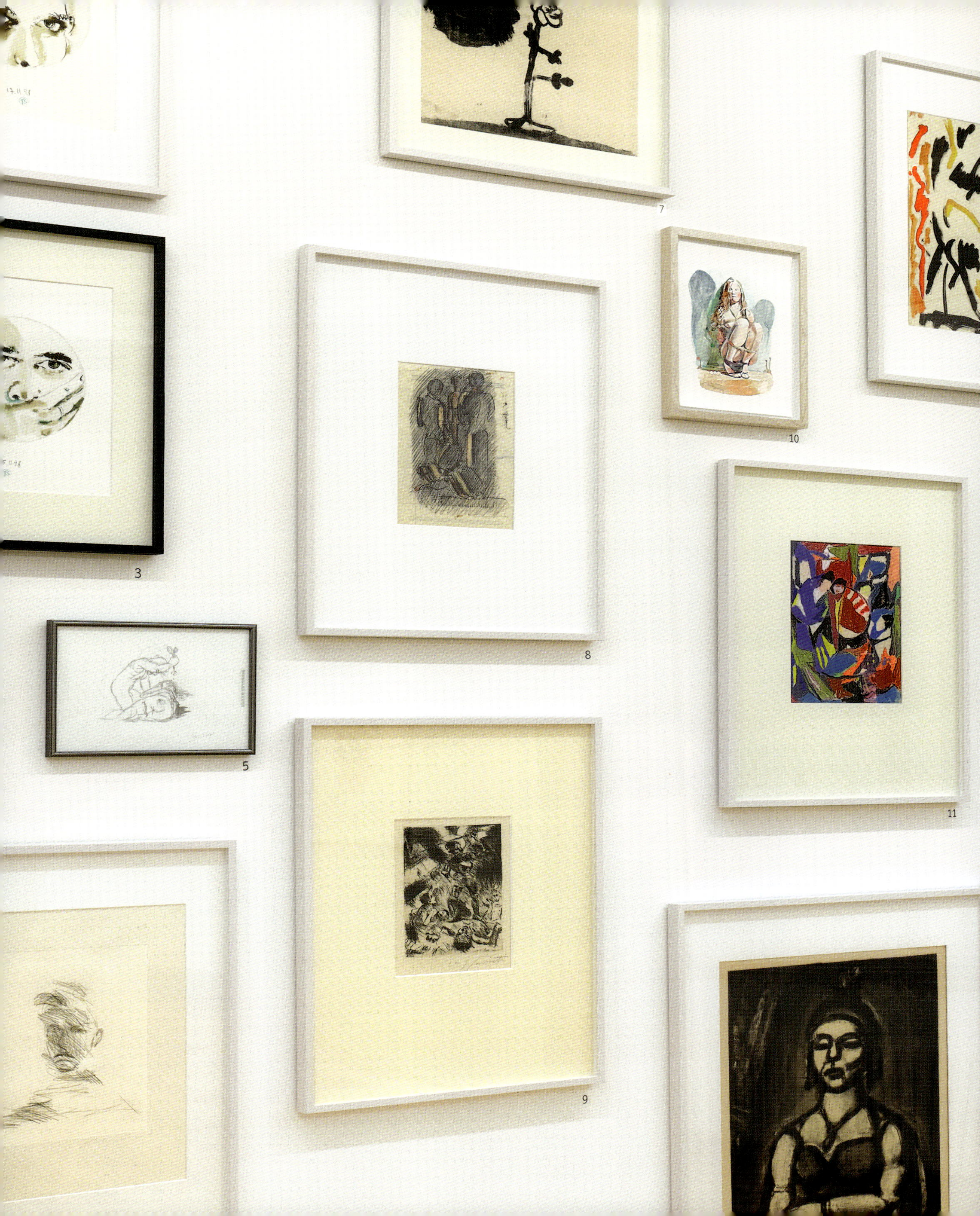
7
10
3
8
5
11
9

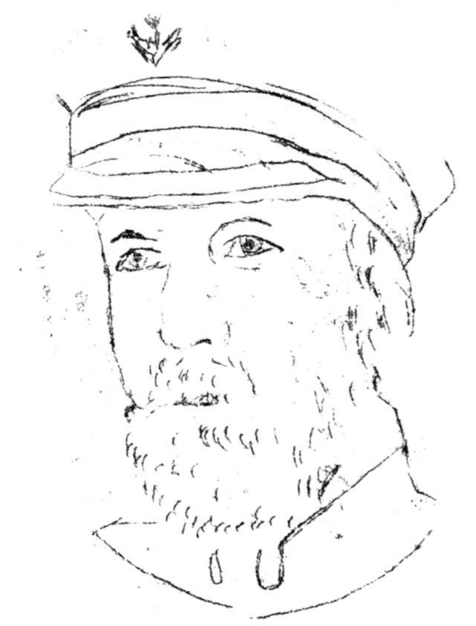

Seh Stück

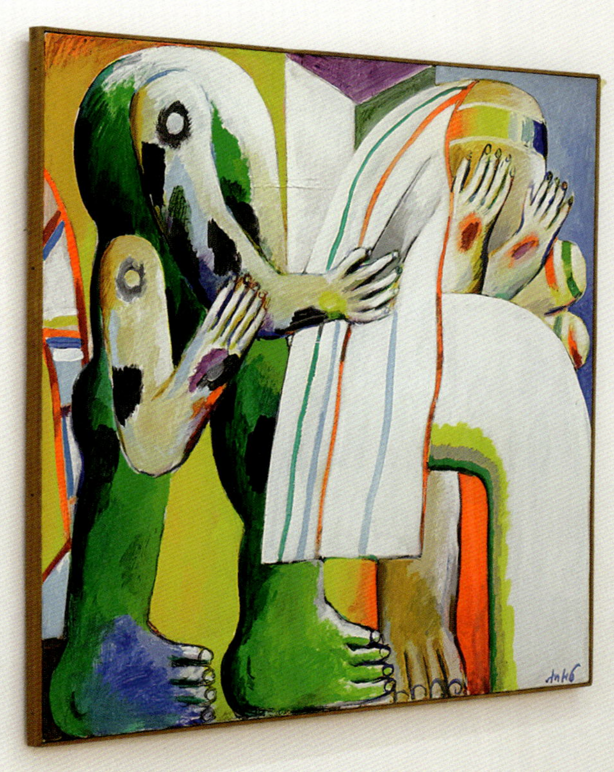

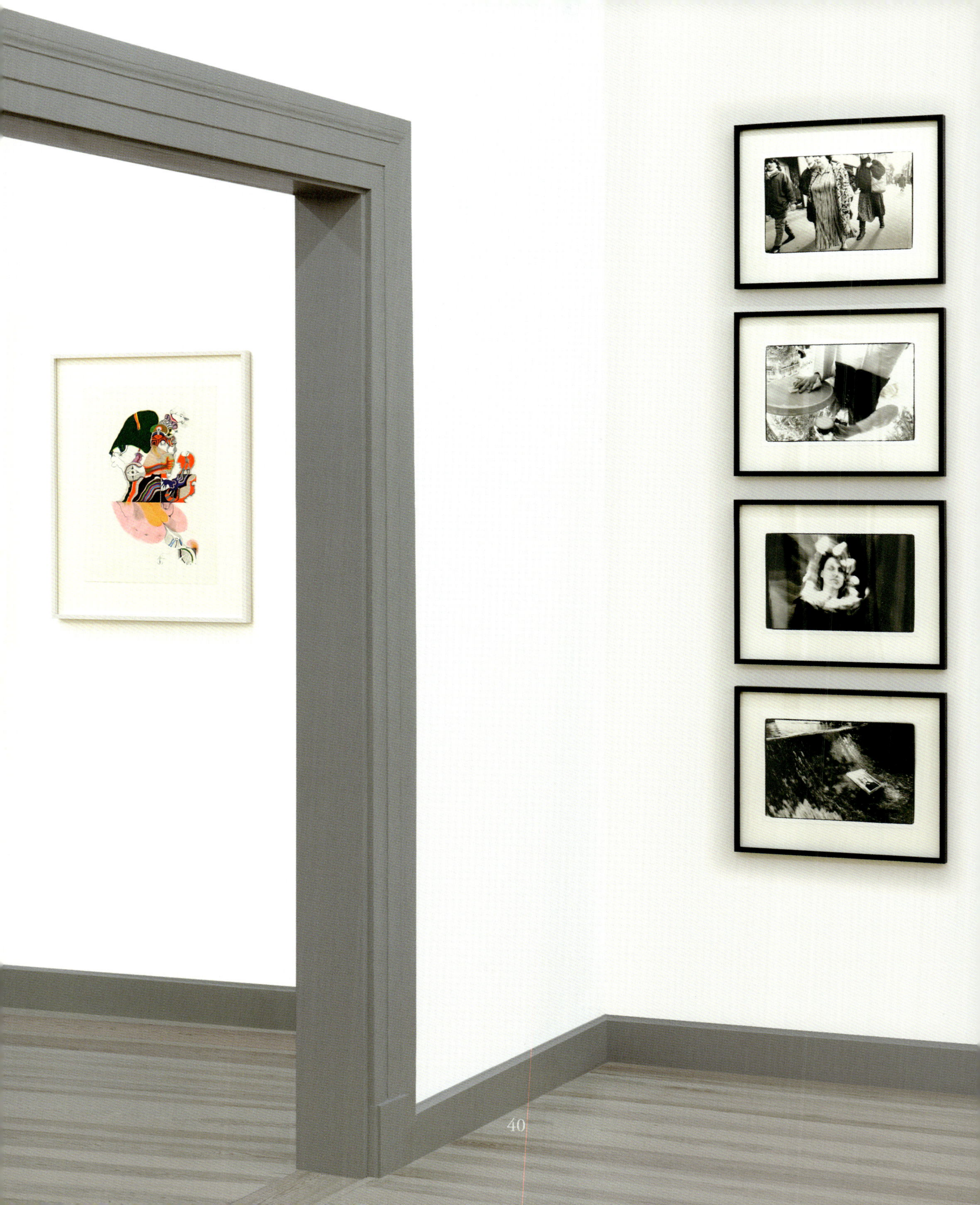

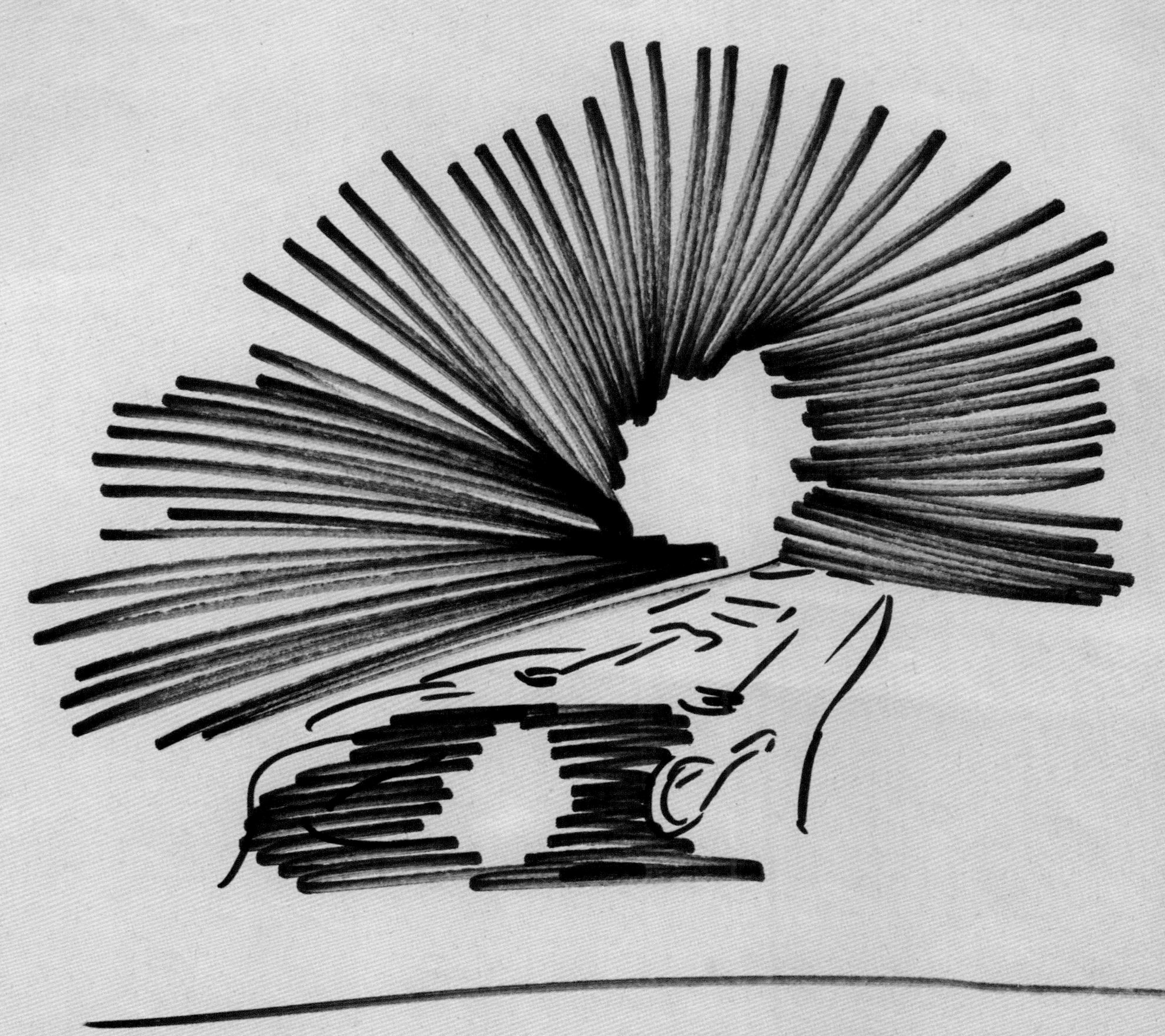

Kosmische Halluzination

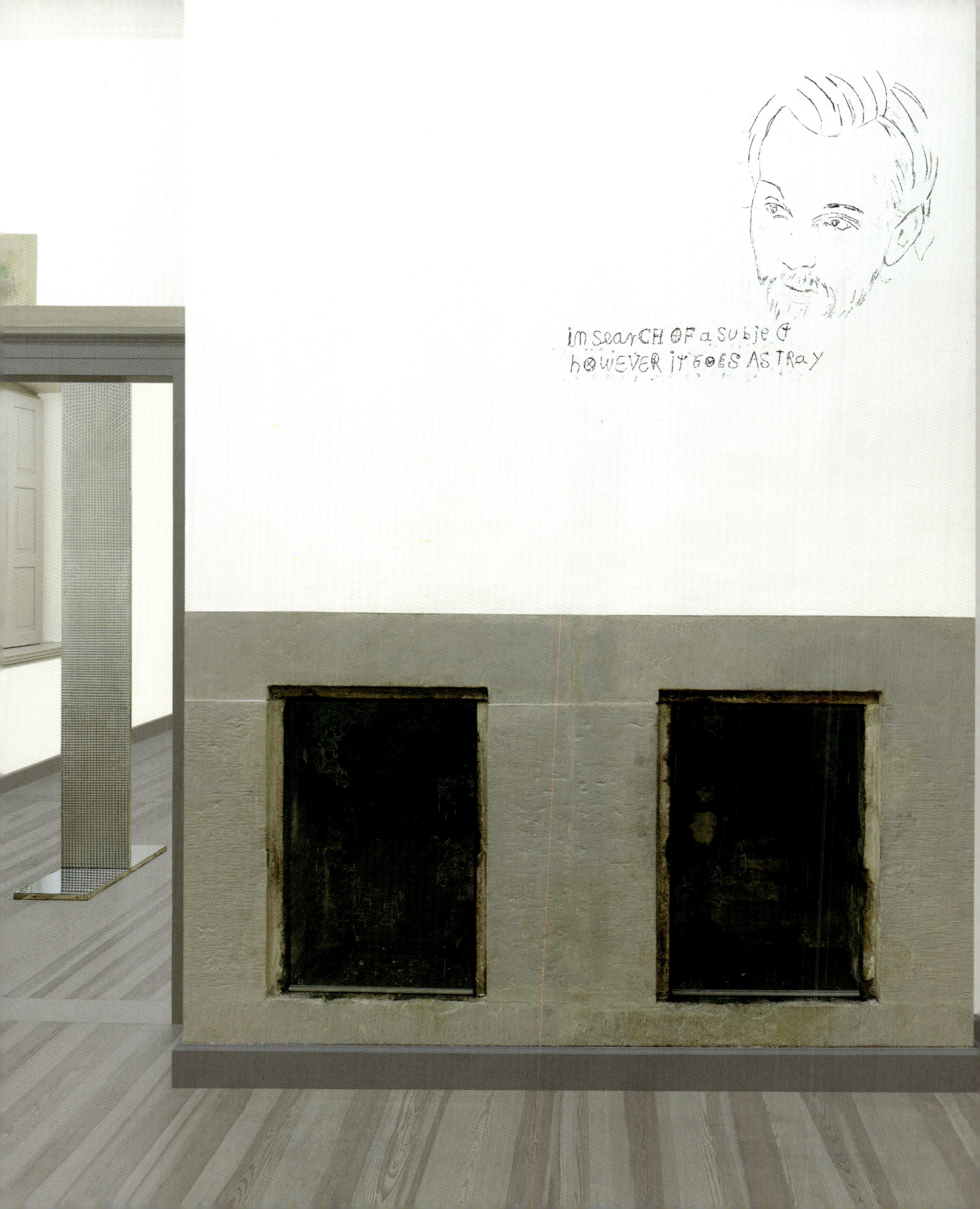

im searCH OF a subje CT
hOWEVER iT GOES ASTRay

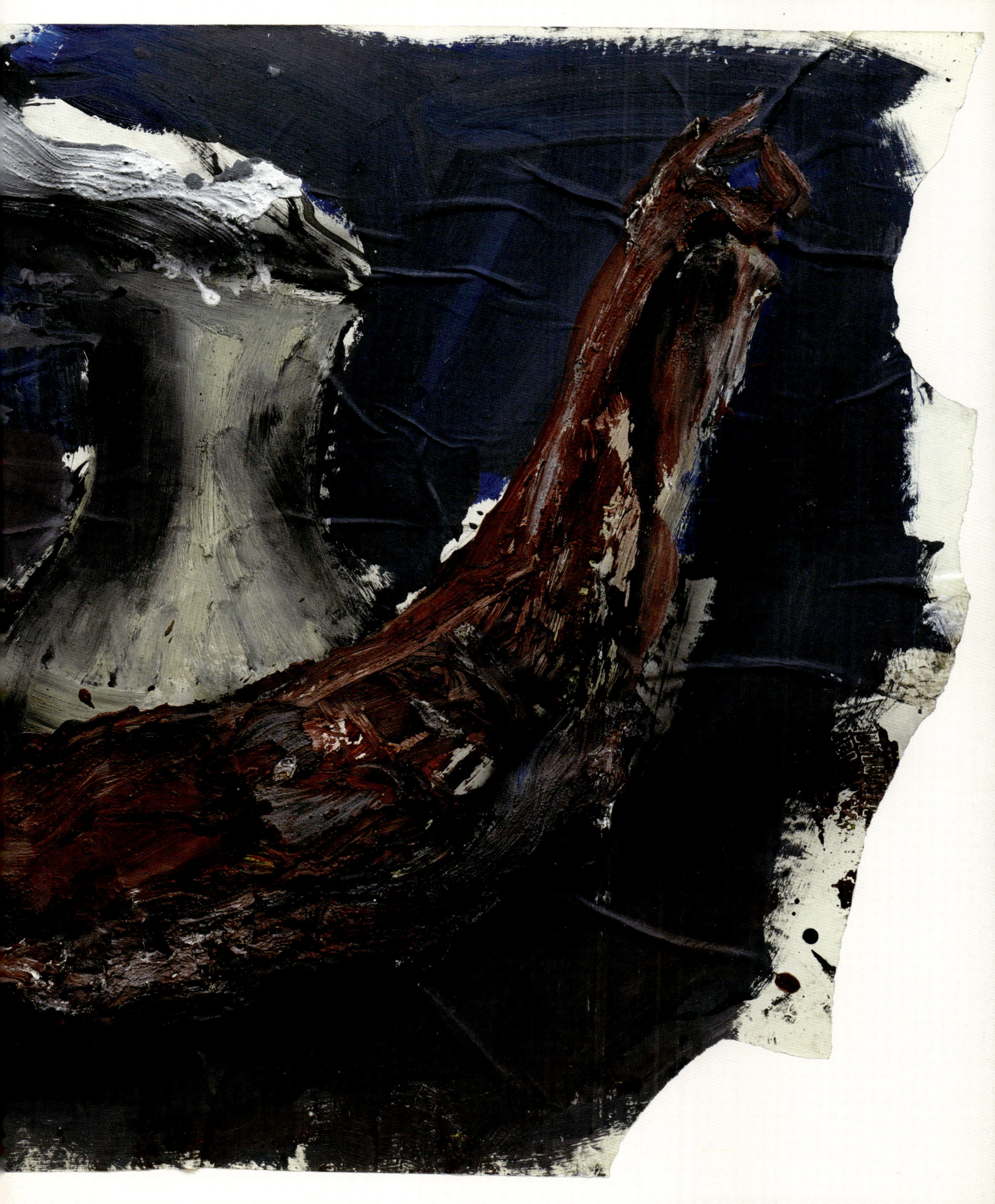

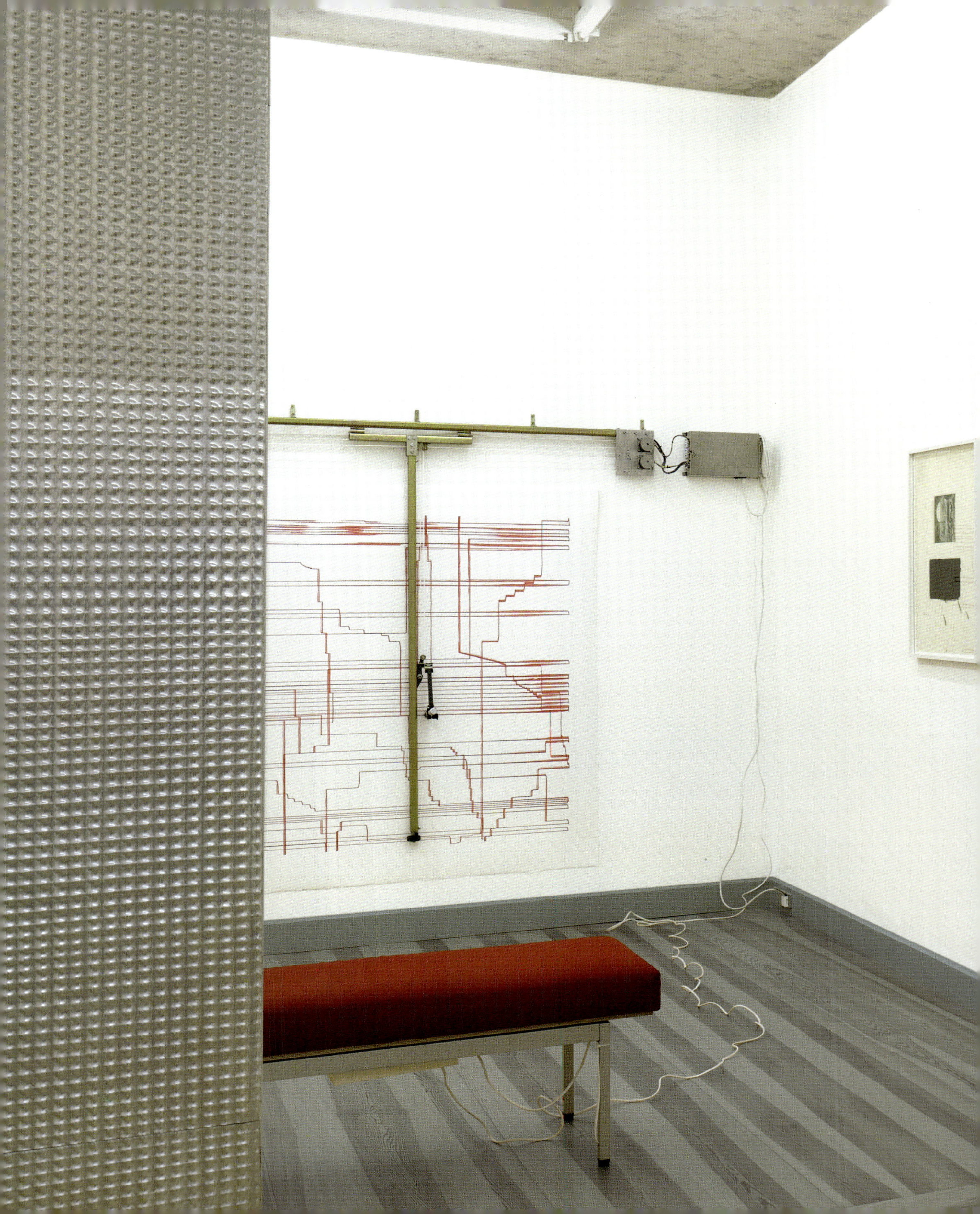

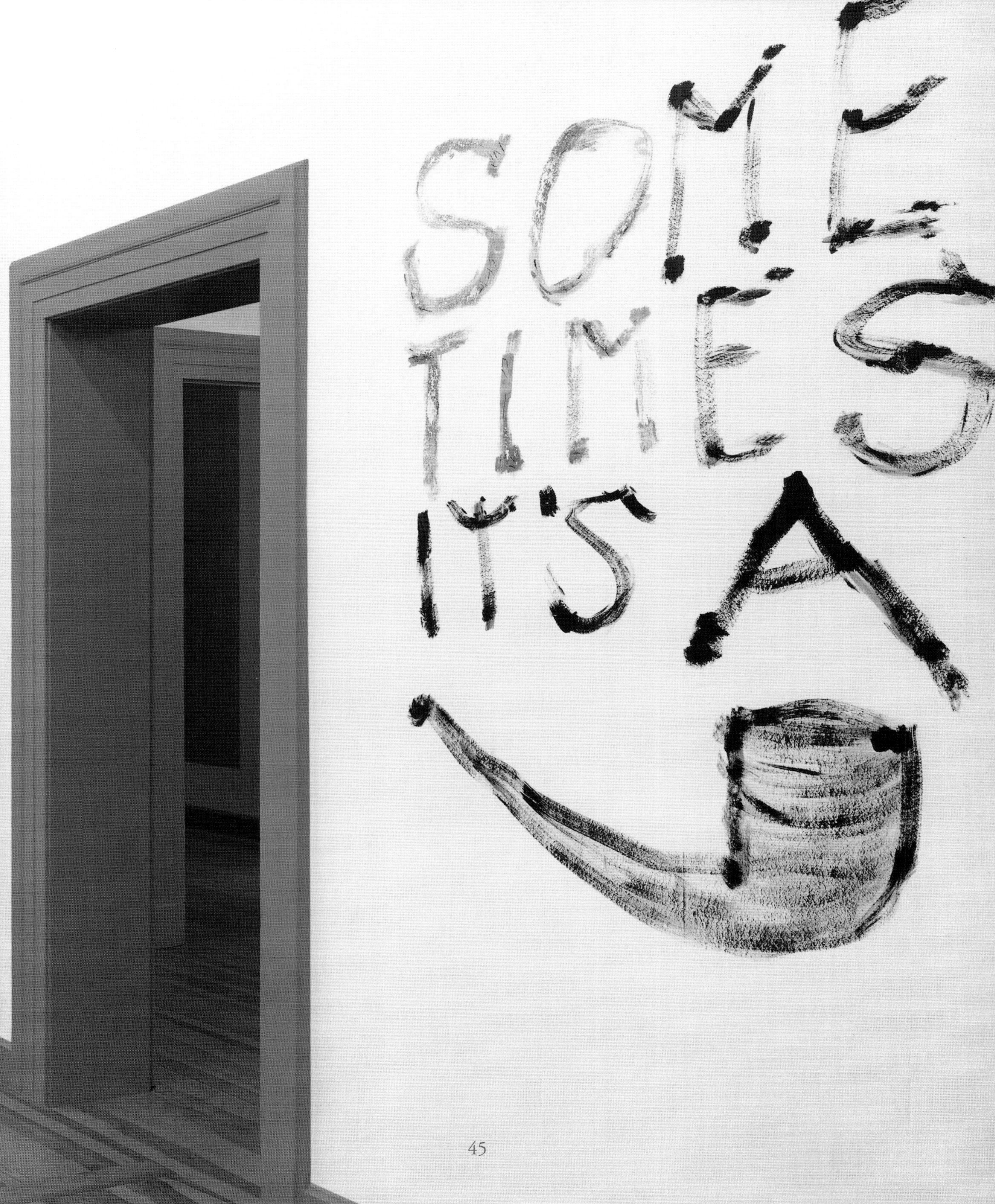
SOME
TIMES
IT'S A

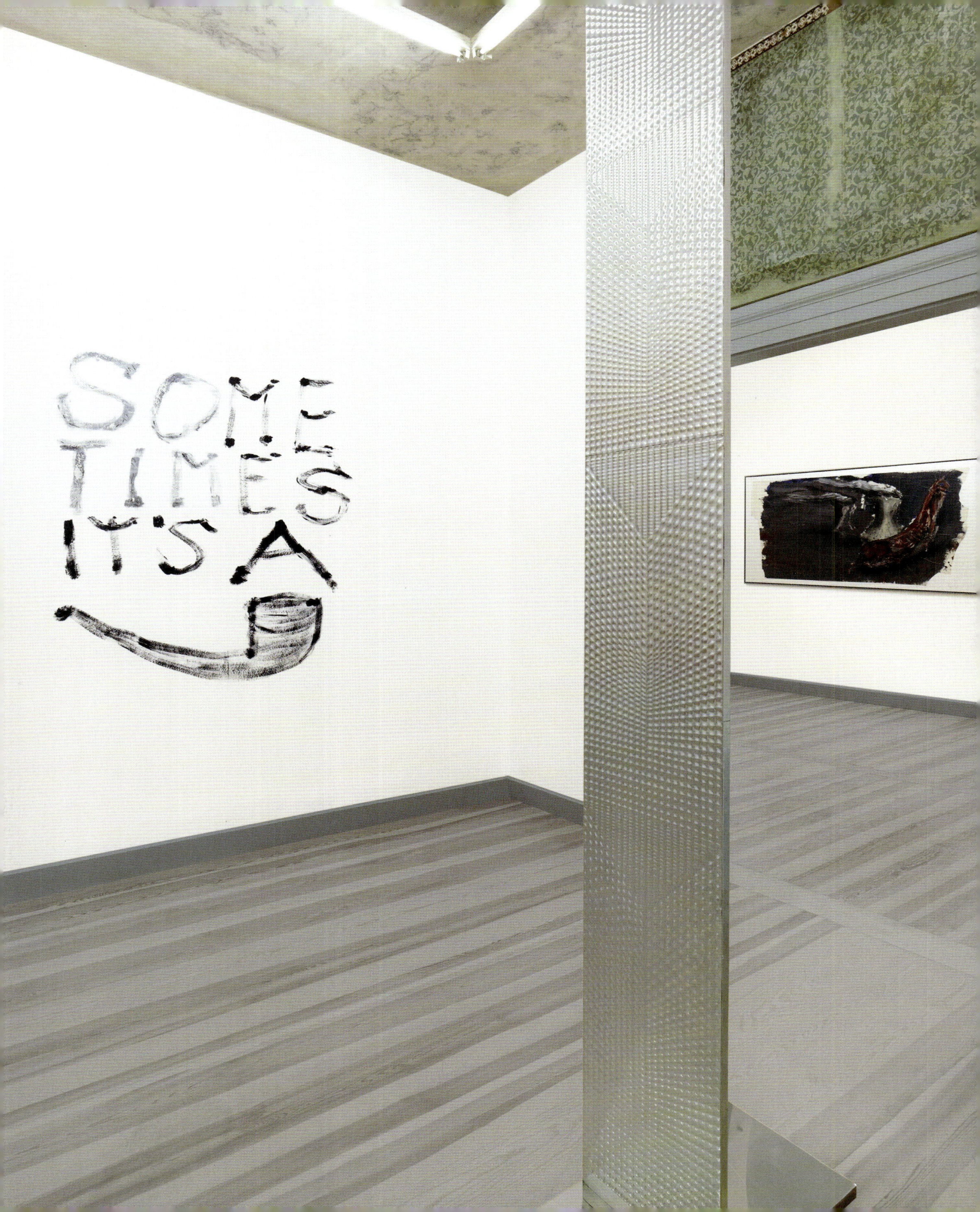
SOME
TIMES
IT'S A

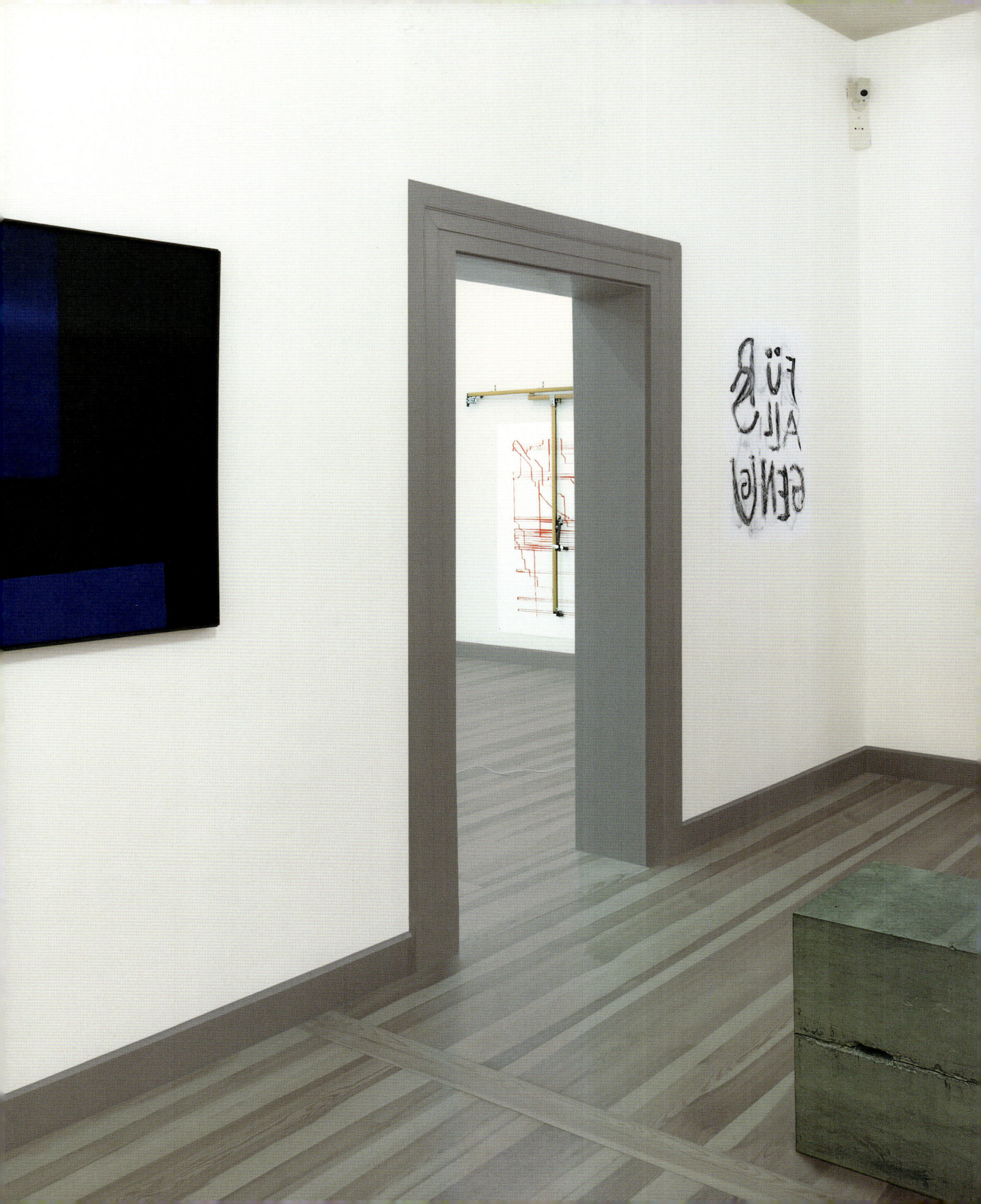

TAKE-OVER

Marcus Körber

Im Mittelpunkt der Aktivitäten der Städtischen Galerie Wolfsburg steht ihre Sammlung moderner und zeitgenössischer Kunst. Seit Beginn der Sammlungstätigkeit in den 1950er-Jahren richtet sich dabei der Fokus auf Kunst aus dem deutschsprachigen Raum nach 1945. Im Bereich der Fotografie, Videokunst und Druckgrafik wurde darüber hinaus schon immer international gesammelt, um die nationale Kunst in einen größeren, will sagen: globalen Kontext mit all seinen Wechselwirkungen einzubetten und für die Besucherinnen und Besucher besser verständlich und visuell erfahrbar zu machen. Damit sei die Zielrichtung, die Absicht und Bestimmung dieser Sammlung kurz und knapp geklärt. Abgehakt und weitermachen wäre nun die Devise. Doch so einfach ist es nicht.
Seit den 1950er-Jahren ist viel Zeit vergangen. Das belegen eindrucksvoll die im Dialog mit dem Künstler Roland Schappert ausgewählten Werke dieser Jubiläumsausstellung zum 40-jährigen Bestehen unseres Museums. Es hat in dieser Zeit, insbesondere durch die rasante Entwicklung digitaler Technologien, gerade im Bereich der neuen Medien, eine völlige Verselbstständigung der Zeichen und Bilder stattgefunden. Einer Sammlung von Bildern, Objekten und Zeichen, wie sie hier in Wolfsburg kontinuierlich aufgebaut wird, fällt nicht zuletzt auch die Aufgabe zu, uns Schaulustige vor dem schleichenden „friendly take-over" einer global agierenden Bildindustrie zu bewahren.

Galerie Wolfsburg's collection of modern and contemporary art lies at the heart of its activities. Since the museum started to collect artworks during the 1950s, its focus has been on art from the post-1945, germanophone world. In addition, there had always been an emphasis on collecting international works from the fields of photography, video and print in order to embed homegrown art into a larger, that is to say, global context and its concomitant interactions and interconnections, as well as to make it more intelligible and visually accessible to the general public. This effectively sums up in a nutshell the overall scope, intention and dispensation of the museum's collection. You might think the motto henceforward would be "done that, now it's time to move on". But it isn't that simple. Many years have elapsed since the 1950s, a fact to which Roland Schappert's dialogue with a selection of works for this anniversary exhibition bears impressive witness, celebrating as it does the museum's fortieth year in existence. During this time, due to rapid growth and development of digital technology, particularly in the field of the new media, the signs and images have veritably taken on an existence of their own. Ultimately, a continually augmented collection of paintings, objects, images and signs, such as this one here in Wolfsburg, is thus charged with the task of preventing us, the curious onlookers, from being engulfed by the gradual "friendly takeover" of a visual industry active on a global scale.

ABBILDUNGSVERZEICHNIS | LIST OF ILLUSTRATIONS

I

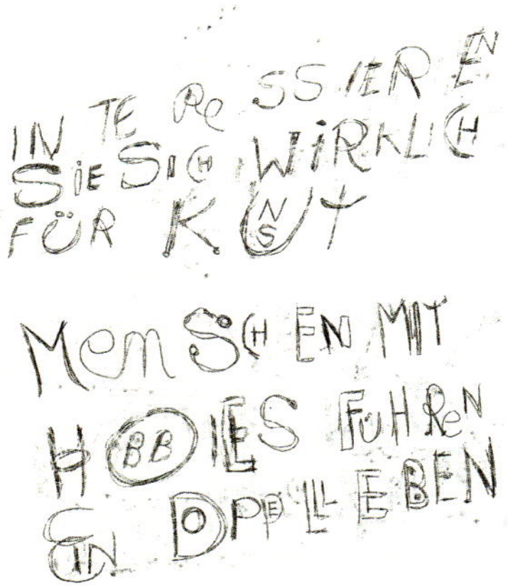

II

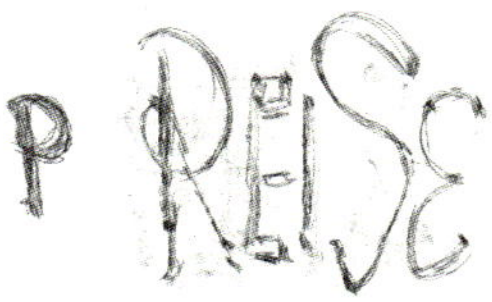

III

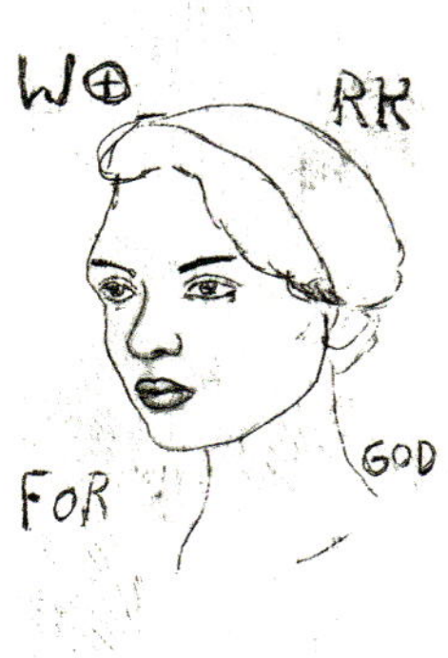

IV

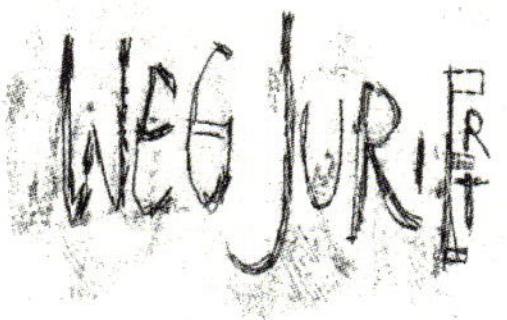

V

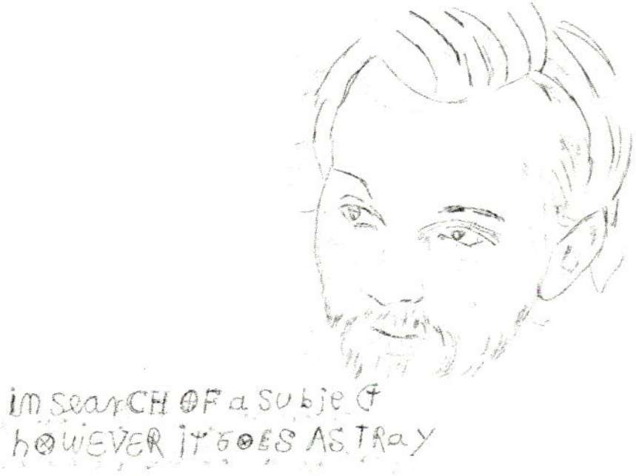

IX

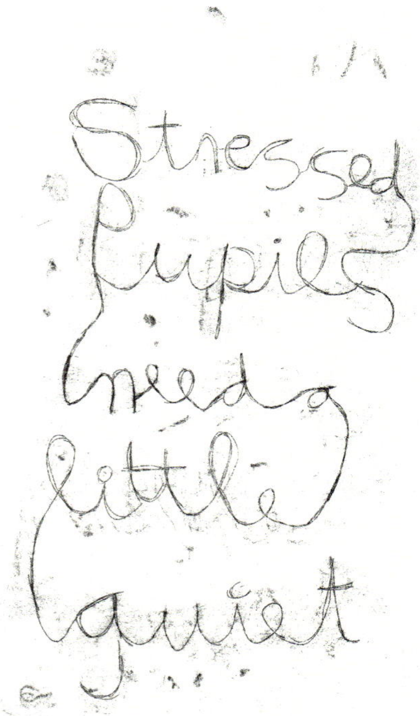

VI

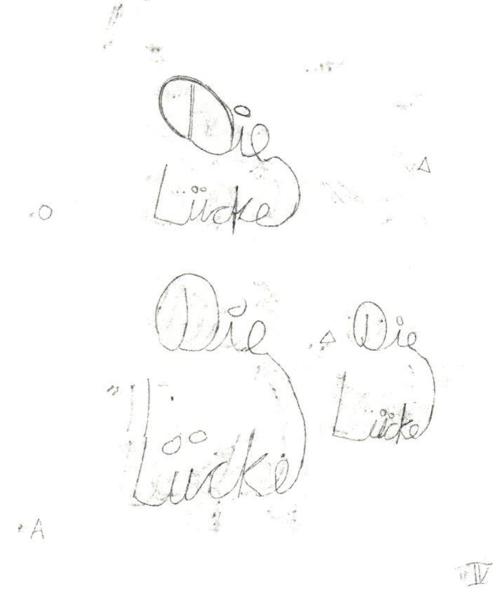

VII

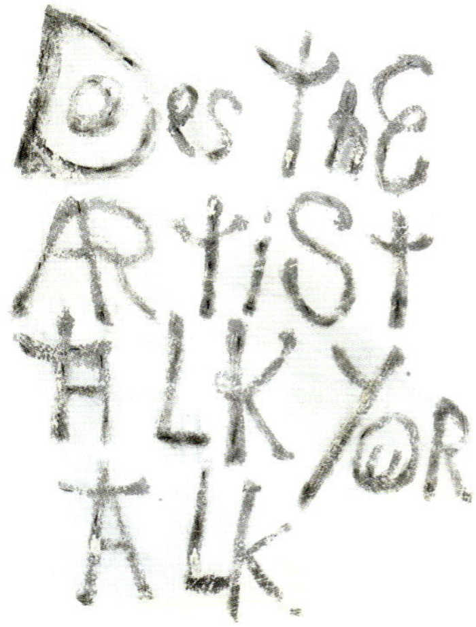

VIII

AUF DER GRUNDsee RaSCH schWANKENDER WERTvoRSTellungen

XI

SORRY

FÜR ABHANDEN GEKOMMENE GEGEN Stände ÜBERNIMMT DIE STADT WOLFSBURG KEINE HAFTUNG

Xa

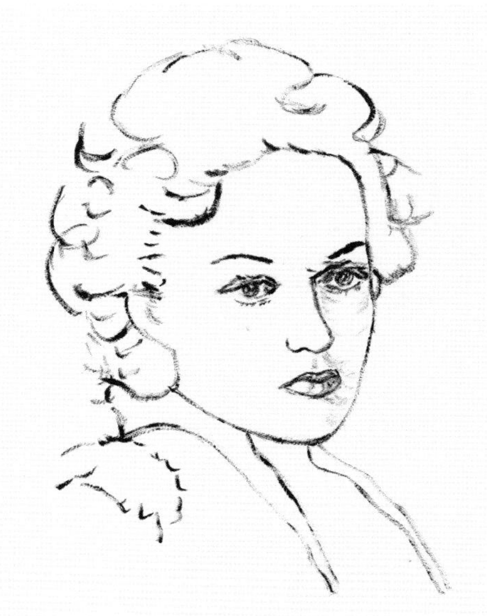

XII

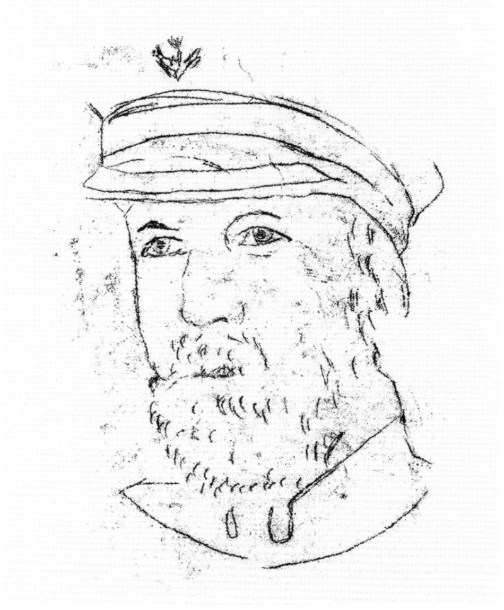

XIIIa

Seh StÜCK

XIIIb

KLEINEIDEEN KRISE

Xb

SONDERN + DAUER IV

KÜNSTLer scheit AUS

HÜbsch aBER UTOPIE

UN VOR SEH BAR

XIV

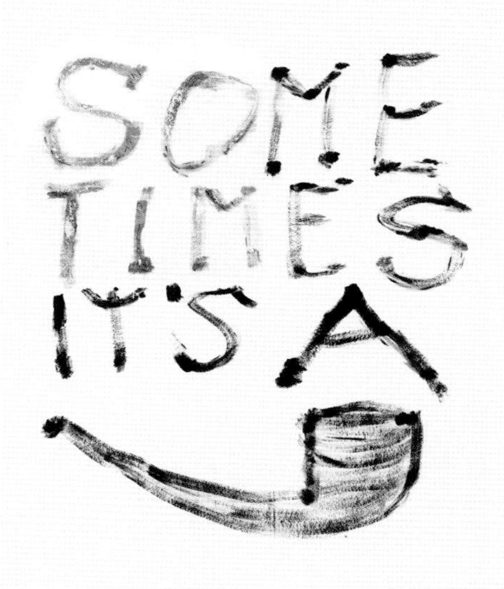

XV

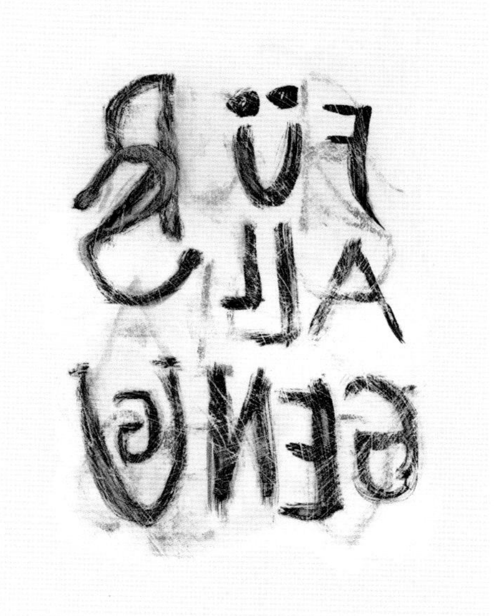

XVI

Seite | page 32
Walter Dahn *1954, Untitled, 1996, Auswahl aus einer Reihe von 6 Zeichnungen, Mischtechnik auf Papier | selection from a series of 6 drawings, mixed media on paper, 29 x 21,5 cm, erworben | acquired 2010.
Seite | page 33
Roland Schappert, SONDERN + DAUER IV / KÜNSTLER SCHERT AUS □ / HÜBSCH ABER UTOPIE A / UN VOR SEH BAR △ | SELECT + DURATION IV / ARTIST VEERS OFF □ / NICE BUT UTOPIAN A / UNFORESEEN △, 2014, 165 x 76 cm.
Seiten | pages 34/35
Roland Schappert, AUF DER GRUNDSEE RASCH SCHWANKENDER WERTVORSTELLUNGEN | GROUNDSWELL OF RAPIDLY VACILLATING MORAL VALUES, 2014, 33 x 530 cm (Detail | detail); KLEINE IDEEN KRISE | MINI CRISIS OF IDEAS, 2014, 10 x 42 cm; SORRY FÜR ABHANDEN GEKOMMENE GEGEN STÄNDE ÜBERNIMMT DIE STADT WOLFSBURG KEINE HAFTUNG | SORRY THE CITY OF WOLFSBURG CANNOT ACCEPT LIABILITY FOR LOST PROPERTY, 2014, 79 x 124 cm.
Seite | page 36
Roland Schappert, o.T. (FRAUENPORTRAIT) | untitled (PORTRAIT OF A WOMAN), 2014, 70 x 50 cm.
Seite | page 37
Thomas Schütte *1954, Ohne Titel, 1998, 2 Tuschfederzeichnungen auf Papier | pen and ink drawing on paper, je | each 39 x 28 cm, erworben | acquired 1999.
Bernhard Martin *1966, Ohne Titel (26.12.07), 2007, Bleistift auf Papier | pencil on paper, 21 x 29,7 cm, erworben | acquired 2009.
Ingeborg Gabriel *1951–1996, Ohne Titel, 1989/1990, Eitempera auf Papier | tempera on paper, 30 x 40 cm, erworben | acquired 1998.
Oskar Schlemmer *1888–1943, Dunkle Gruppe, 1937, Farbstiftzeichnung auf Papier | coloured pencil on paper, 28,5 x 20 cm, erworben | acquired 1965.
Lovis Corinth *1858–1925, Jüngstes Gericht, aus der Mappe „Kunst der Gegenwart" der Marées-Gesellschaft um 1925, Radierung auf Büttenpapier | from the Marees Gesellschaft's "Kunst der Gegenwart" portfolio, c. 1925, drypoint on wove paper, 34,5 x 27,5 cm, erworben | acquired 1991.
Adolf Hoelzel *1853–1934, Figürliche Komposition, 1923–1928, Pastellfarben auf Papier | pastels on paper, 33 x 25 cm, erworben | acquired 1966.
Caro Suerkemper *1964, Ohne Titel, 2008, Gouache auf Papier | gouache on paper, 31 x 23 cm, erworben | acquired 2008.
Georges Rouault *1871–1958, Des Ongles et du Bec, 1926, Heliogravüre und Radierung auf Büttenpapier | photogravure and drypoint etching on wove paper (9/17), 57,5 x 44,5 cm auf | on 65 x 50,5 cm, erworben | acquired 1964.
Ernst Ludwig Kirchner *1880–1938, Frauenakt, 1905, Mischtechnik auf Papier | mixed media on paper, 45 x 35,2 cm erworben | acquired 1965.
Alberto Giacometti *1901–1966, Arthur Rimbaud (vu par les peintres), 1962, Radierung auf Papier (E.A.) | etching on paper (a.p.), 56,5 x 45 cm, erworben 1996.
Seite | page 38
Jürgen Klauke *1943, Melancholie der Stühle, 1981, Fotografie 17-teilig | photograph in seventeen parts, 180 x 190 cm (Detail | detail), erworben | acquired 1983.
Roland Schappert, o.T. (MÄNNERPORTRAIT) | untitled (PORTRAIT OF A MAN), 2014, 57 x 37 cm; Seh STÜCK | See SCAPE, 2014, 12 x 29 cm.
Seite | page 39
Roland Schappert, Seh STÜCK | See SCAPE
→ Seite | page 38.
Horst Antes *1936, Kleines Hochzeitsbild, 1965/1966, Öl auf Leinwand | oil on canvas, 102 x 112 cm, erworben | acquired 1967.
Seite | page 40
Steffen Lucht *1941, Zeichnung III, 1967, Bleistift und Farbkreide auf Bütten | pencil and coloured chalk on wove paper, 56 x 42 cm, erworben | acquired 1967.
Evgen Bavcar *1946, Die biographische Sequenz, 1980–1986, Auswahl an Fotografien | selection of photographs, 20 x 30 cm, erworben | acquired 1992.
Seite | page 41
Bernhard Johannes Blume *1937–2011, ohne Titel, 1976/1977, Auswahl aus 10 Filzstiftzeichnungen auf Papier zu „Schizo" | selection of 10 drawings in felt pen on paper relating to "Schizo", je | each 29,7 x 21 cm, erworben | acquired 1983.
Seite | page 42
Heinz Mack *1931, One becomes two, 1965, Lichtstele aus Aluminium und Holz | light stele, aluminium and wood, 293 x 34,5 cm, erworben | acquired 1971.
Roland Schappert, o.T. (MÄNNERPORTRAIT) / IN SEARCH OF A SUBJECT HOWEVER IT GOES ASTRAY | untitled (PORTRAIT OF A MAN) / IN SEARCH OF A SUBJECT HOWEVER IT GOES ASTRAY, 2014, 92 x 117 cm.
Seite | page 43
Dieter Krieg *1937–2005, Ohne Titel, 1984, Acryl auf Papier auf Leinwand | acrylic on paper on canvas, 100 x 200 cm (Detail | detail), erworben | acquired 2014.
Seiten | pages 44/45
Heinz Mack, One becomes two (Detail | detail)
→ Seite | page 42

Angela Bulloch *1966, Constructostrato Drawing Machine (red), 2011, Sitzbank, Tinte, Metallschiene, Elektromotor, Papier | bench, ink, metal rails, electric motor, paper; Blatt | sheet 152 x 250 cm, Maschine | machine 160 x 330 cm, Bank | bench 45 x 45 x 144 cm, erworben | acquired 2011.
Arnulf Rainer *1929, Übermalung Pape, 1961, Tempera auf Kupferradierung | tempera on copper etching, 12,5 x 24,7 cm (66,5 x 51,5 cm), erworben | acquired 1973.
Roland Schappert, SOMETIMES IT'S A / o.T. (PFEIFEN-PORTRAIT) | SOMETIMES IT'S A / untitled (PIPE PORTRAIT), 2014, 145 x 130 cm.

Seite | page 46
Roland Schappert, SOMETIMES IT'S A / o.T. (PFEIFEN-PORTRAIT) | SOMETIMES IT'S A / untitled (PIPE PORTRAIT) → Seite | page 45.
Heinz Mack, One becomes two (Detail | detail) → Seite | page 42.
Dieter Krieg, Ohne Titel → Seite | page 43.

Seite | page 47
Rupprecht Geiger *1908–2009, Zweimal Blau auf Schwarz Nr. 354, 1961, Öl auf Leinwand | oil on canvas, 91,5 x 122 cm, erworben | acquired 1962.
Angela Bulloch, Constructostrato Drawing Machine (red) → Seite | page 44.
Roland Schappert, FÜRS ALL GENUG | ENOUGH FOR THE UNIVERSE, 2014, 90 x 63 cm.
Ulrich Rückriem *1938, Grüner Dolomit, 1977, Steinquader gespalten | blocks of stone, split, 40 x 40 x 50 cm, erworben | acquired 1981.

Seiten | pages 50/51
Übersicht der in der Ausstellung gezeigten Wandmalereien von Roland Schappert | Overview of Roland Schappert's murals shown in the exhibition: I → Seite | page 13; II → Seite | page 17; III → Seite | page 18; IV → Seite | page 24; V → Seite | page 26; VI → Seite | page 14; VII → Seite | page 21; VIII → Seite | page 30; IX → Seite | page 42; Xa → Seite | page 35; Xb → Seite | page 35; XI → Seite | page 34; XII → Seite | page 36; XIIIa → Seite | page 38; XIIIb → Seite | page 38; XIV → Seite | page 33; XV → Seite | page 45; XVI → Seite | page 47.

Cover
Roland Schappert, FÜRS ALL GENUG | ENOUGH FOR THE UNIVERSE → Seite | page 47.

Seiten | pages 4/5
Roland Schappert, DOES THE ARTIST TALK YOUR TALK (Detail | detail) → Seite | page 28; Seite 5 unter Verwendung des Ausstellungsflyers nach dem Design von | page 5 makes use of the exhibition flyer designed by Markus Dreßen, Leipzig.

Die im Folgenden genannten Arbeiten sind speziell für den vorliegenden Katalog entstanden | The following works have been made especially for this catalogue:

Seiten | pages 2/3
Roland Schappert, WOZU SAMMELN / LOVE IT | WHY COLLECT / LOVE IT, Kugelschreiberzeichnung auf abgesofteten Ansichten der Städtischen Galerie Wolfsburg, Fotografien: Simon Vogel | ball-point drawing on softened images of the Städtische Galerie Wolfsburg, photos: Simon Vogel, 2014.

Seite | page 6
Roland Schappert, ARTTermostat | ARTTermostat, Kugelschreiberzeichnung | ball-point drawing, 2015.

Seite | page 35
Roland Schappert, ee RaSCH SCHWANKenDER WERtVORSteLLUNGEN | ELL OF RAPIDLY VACILLATING MORAL VALUES, Kugelschreiberzeichnung | ball-point drawing, 2014.

Seiten | pages 54/55
Roland Schappert, WENN DU FÜR ETWAS STEHST HEUTE / BIST DU VERDÄCHTIG | YOU AROUSE SUSPICION / NOWADAYS IF YOU STAND FOR SOMETHING, Kugelschreiberzeichnung auf abgesofteten Ansichten der Städtischen Galerie Wolfsburg, Fotografien: Simon Vogel | ball-point drawing on softened images of the Städtische Galerie Wolfsburg, photos: Simon Vogel, 2014.

Backcover
Lienhard von Monkiewitsch, Grüner Fußboden (Detail | detail) → Seite | page 15, auf abgesofteter Ansicht der Städtischen Galerie Wolfsburg, Fotografien: Simon Vogel | on softened image of the Städtische Galerie Wolfsburg, photos: Simon Vogel, 2014.

Alle Wandmalereien von Roland Schappert: Siebdruck- und Fluo-Vinylfarben auf Wandfarbe oder Marmor-Sumpfkalkfarbe | All wall paintings by Roland Schappert: screenprint and flourescent vinyl paint or marble dust limewash.

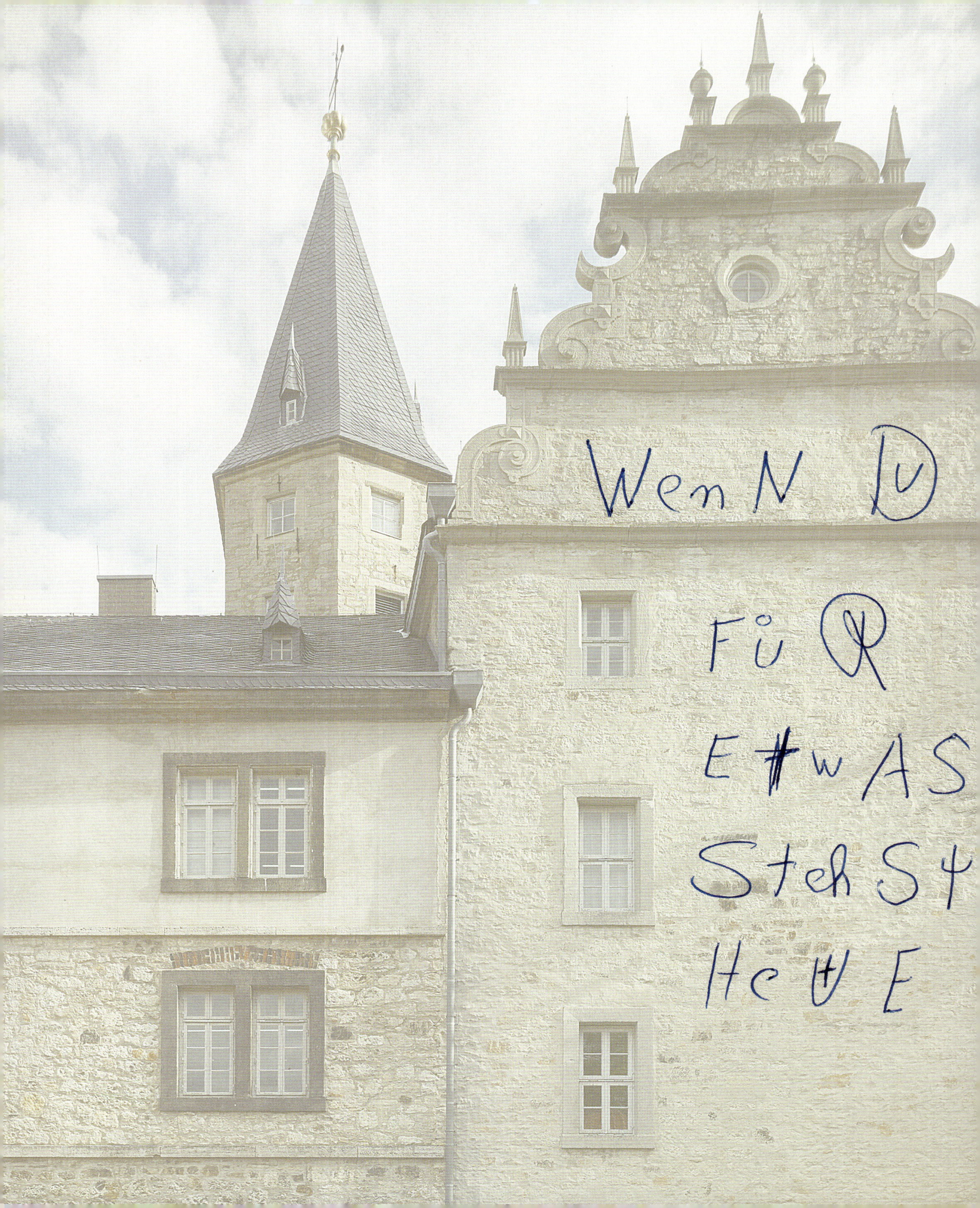
WenN DU
FüR
EtwAS
SteHSt
HeUtE

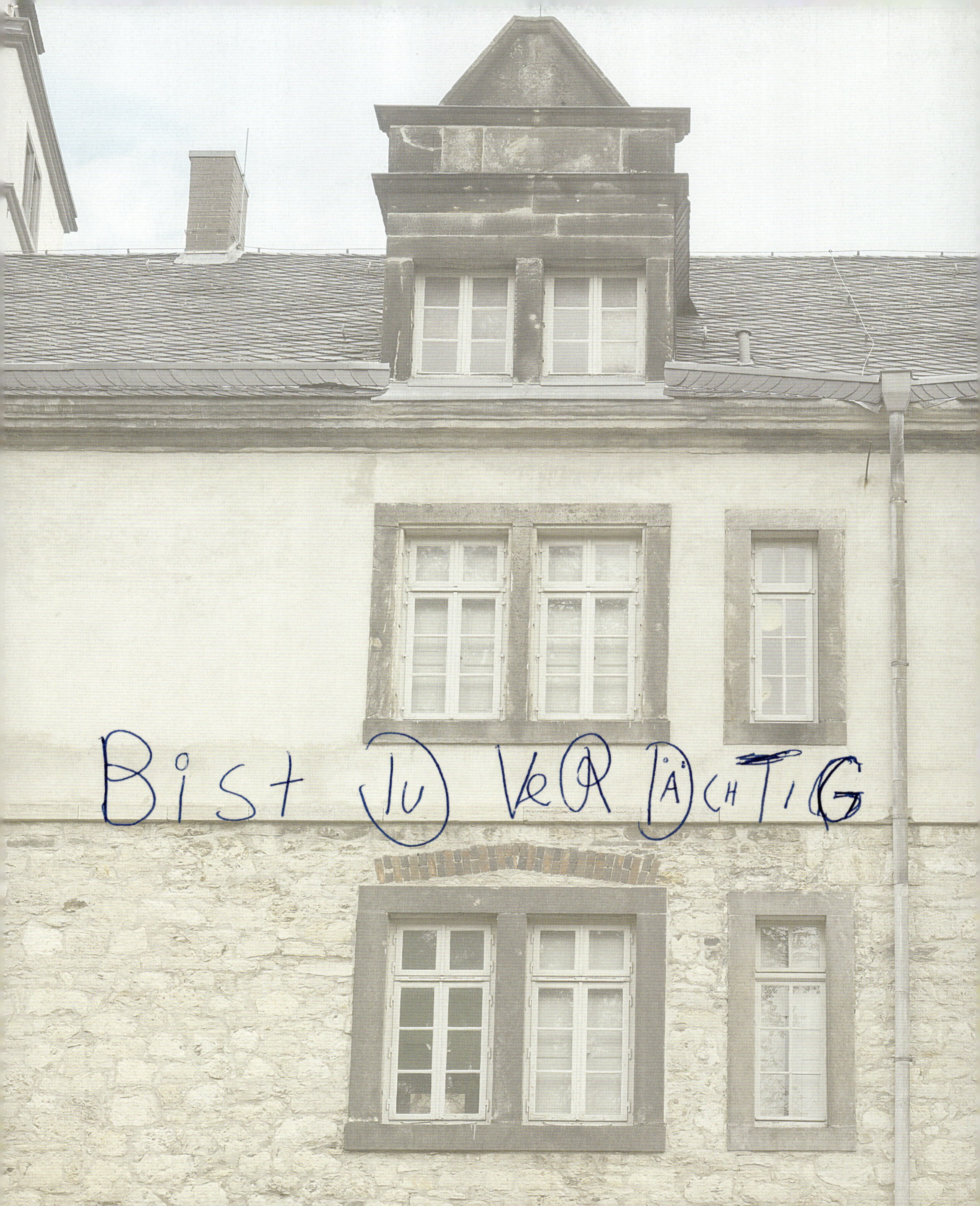
Bist du verdächtig

ROLAND SCHAPPERT, *1965, arbeitet als Maler an den Grenzbereichen der Medien.
1993–1995 Graduiertenstipendium zur Förderung des wissenschaftlichen und künstlerischen Nachwuchses des Landes NRW. 2005 erhielt Roland Schappert mit Michael Ebmeyer den Videonale-Preis im Kunstmuseum Bonn. 2007–2010 Gastprofessor für Malerei und das Malerische in den Medien an der Hochschule für Bildende Künste Braunschweig. Veröffentlichungen, Vorträge und Performances zu Aspekten eines zeitgenössischen Kunstbegriffs, Kunst und Wirtschaft.

Born in 1965, ROLAND SCHAPPERT is a painter whose work pushes the boundaries of conventional media.
1993–1995 post graduate scholarship of the Land North Rhine-Westphalia for the promotion of young scientific and artistic talent. In 2005 Roland Schappert and Michael Ebmeyer were jointly awarded the Videonale Award at the Kunstmuseum Bonn. 2007–2010 visiting professor of painting and painterly aspects of media at Braunschweig University of Art. Publications, lectures and performances on aspects of a contemporary conception of art, art and business.

Impressum | Colophon

FÜRS ALL GENUG
Werke aus der Sammlung im Dialog mit Wandmalereien von Roland Schappert – 40 Jahre Städtische Galerie Wolfsburg, 21. Oktober 2014 bis 30. August 2015

Dieser Katalog erscheint anlässlich der Ausstellung FÜRS ALL GENUG in der Städtischen Galerie Wolfsburg. | This catalogue is published on the occasion of the exhibition FÜRS ALL GENUG in Städtische Galerie Wolfsburg.

Herausgeber | Editors: Susanne Pfleger, Marcus Körber
Konzeption | Concept: Roland Schappert, Marcus Körber
Gestaltung | Design: Heinrich Miess, Köln
(Seite 5 unter Verwendung des Ausstellungsflyers nach dem Design von | page 5 makes use of the exhibition flyer designed by Markus Dreßen, Leipzig)
Übersetzungen | Translations: Tim Connell, London
Lektorat | Copy editing: Winfried Stürzl, Stuttgart
Fotonachweis | Photo credits: Simon Vogel, Köln
Gesamtherstellung | Production: Steinmeier, Deiningen

Die Deutsche Nationalbibliothek verzeichnet diese Publikation in der Deutschen Nationalbibliografie; detaillierte bibliografische Daten sind im Internet über http://dnb.dnb.de abrufbar.
The Deutsche Nationalbibliothek lists this publication in the Deutsche Nationalbibliografie; detailed bibliographic data are available in the Internet at http://dnb.dnb.de.

ISBN 978-3-95476-098-5
Printed in Germany

Vertrieb | Distribution
Gestalten, Berlin
www.gestalten.com
sales@gestalten.com

Erschienen im | Published by
DISTANZ Verlag
www.distanz.de

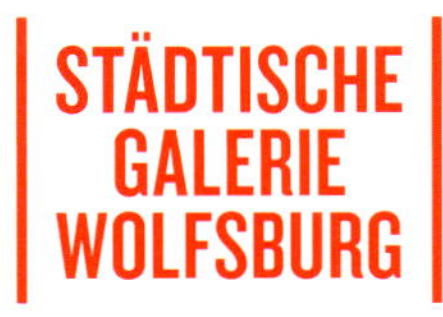

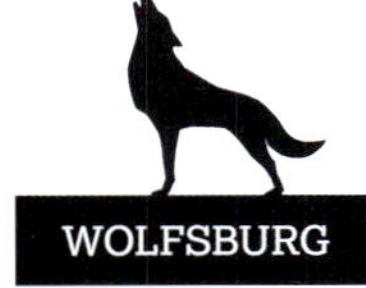